Easy Windows™

Shelley O'Hara

Easy Windows™

Copyright © 1991 by Que® Corporation.

Library of Congress Catalog No.: 91-62461

ISBN: 0-88022-800-8

93 92 91   6 5 4 3 2 1

Interpretation of the printing code: the rightmost double-digit number is the year of the book's printing; the rightmost single-digit number, the number of the book's printing. For example, a printing code of 91-1 shows that the first printing of the book occurred in 1991.

Screen reproductions in this book were created using Collage Plus from Inner Media, Inc., Hollis, NH.

Easy Windows is based on Microsoft Windows Version 3.0.

Publisher: Lloyd J. Short

Associate Publisher: Karen A. Bluestein

Product Development Manager: Mary Bednarek

Managing Editor: Paul Boger

Book Designers: Scott Cook, Karen A. Bluestein

Illustrations: Scott Cook

Production Team: Beth J. Baker, Sandy Grieshop, Bob LaRoche, Michele Laseau

Series Director
Karen A. Bluestein

Project Leader
Kathie-Jo Arnoff

Production Editor
Cindy Morrow

Editor
Patricia A. Brooks

Technical Editor
Timothy S. Stanley

Novice Reviewer
Janis Fechalos

Contents at a Glance

Easy Windows

Contents

Easy Windows

Contents

Easy **Windows**

Introduction

Microsoft Windows is a graphical user interface or a GUI (pronounced "gooey") that changes the way you use your computer. When you start a computer that does not have a GUI, you usually see only a two- or three-character prompt (perhaps C:\>) and a blank screen. To copy files, use programs, or make the computer work, you must type commands. And you must type the commands in the proper format (this format is sometimes called *syntax*).

This method of using a program requires that you memorize many different commands and type them correctly when you want to use the computer. Microsoft Windows makes using a computer easier.

Microsoft Windows uses a desktop metaphor. In other words, rather than displaying a blank screen when you start, Microsoft Windows displays a desktop with windows and icons. (Icons are pictures that represent other windows or programs.) This visual approach enables you to point to what you want. Starting a program, for example, is simply a matter of pointing at what you want and clicking the mouse. (See *Using the Mouse* in the Basics part.)

With Microsoft Windows you can:

Start programs. Rather than memorize and type commands to start a program, you point to the icon of the program that you want and click the mouse. The program opens on-screen in a window.

Manage files. You can use Microsoft Windows to display files, copy files, move files, rename files, and perform other file-management tasks. You can select commands from a menu, rather than type them. You can display files in a window on-screen, and you can display several of these windows at once.

Use Microsoft Windows desk accessories. Included with Microsoft Windows are a color paint program, a word processor, a calendar, a calculator, a notepad, a cardfile, two games, and other programs. You can use these programs to draw logos, create documents, schedule appointments, solve equations, type notes, store addresses, and have fun.

Display more than one window at a time. When you work on a project, you don't just have one sheet of paper on your desk—you have several. One sheet might contain sales projections; one might be your current inventory list; one might be notes from sales representatives. You use all these pieces of information to create a report. Working with Microsoft Windows is the same way. You can display the information that you need in several windows and then move among the windows.

Run two programs at once. If your computer has enough memory, you can run two programs at once and switch between them. You can enter figures in a worksheet and then pull those figures into a word-processing document. (This book does not cover this more advanced feature.)

Use Microsoft Windows-based programs. Many programs are designed specifically to work with Microsoft Windows. These programs all essentially work the same way. After you learn one Microsoft Windows program, you can learn other Microsoft Windows programs easily.

Why You Need This Book

All of Microsoft Windows' features make working with your computer easy. Using this program saves you time and makes your work more efficient. But learning to use the many features is difficult at first, which is why you need this book.

This book is designed to make learning Microsoft Windows *easy*. This book helps the beginning Microsoft Windows user perform basic operations. Following the step-by-step instructions, you can learn to take advantage of Microsoft Windows' functions and capabilities.

You don't need to worry that your knowledge of computers or Microsoft Windows is too limited to use the program well. This book teaches you all that you need to know to get started in Microsoft Windows.

Reading this book will build your confidence. It will show you what steps are necessary to get a particular job done.

How This Book Is Organized

This book is designed with you, the beginner, in mind. It is divided into several parts:

- Introduction
- The Basics
- Task/Review
- Reference

This Introduction explains how the book is set up and how you can use it.

The next part, The Basics, outlines general information about your computer and its keyboard layout. This part explains basic concepts, such as using the mouse, selecting commands, and understanding the Microsoft Windows display.

The main portion of this book, Task/Review, tells you how to perform specific tasks. Each task includes numbered steps that tell you what to do to complete a specific sample exercise. Before and After screens illustrate the exercise.

The last part, Reference, contains a glossary of common computer terms and explains how those terms apply to Microsoft Windows. This part also contains a quick reference, which shows you tasks and the steps to perform a task at a glance. Finally, the reference part contains an appendix that explains how to use a keyboard in Microsoft Windows, if you don't have a mouse.

How To Use This Book

This book is set up so that you can use it several different ways:

- You can read the book from start to finish.

- You can start reading at any point in the book.

- You can experiment with one exercise, many exercises, or all exercises.

- You can look up specific tasks that you want to accomplish, such as moving a window.

- You can flip through the book, looking at the Before and After screens, to find specific tasks.

- You can read only the exercise, only the review, or both the exercise and review sections. As you learn the program, you might want to follow along with the exercises. After you learn the program, you can refer back to the Review to remind yourself how to perform a specific task.

- You can read any part of the exercises that you want. You can read all the text to see both the steps to follow and the explanation of the steps. You can read only the text in red to see only the commands to select. You can read only the explanation to understand what happens during a particular step.

Task section

The Task section includes numbered steps that tell you how to accomplish certain tasks, such as resizing a window or copying a file. The numbered steps walk you through a specific example so that you can learn the task by doing it. Blue text below the numbered steps explains the concept in more detail.

Oops! notes

You may find that you performed a task that you do not want after all. The Oops! notes tell you how to undo each procedure or explain how to get out of a situation. By showing you how to reverse nearly every procedure or get out of nearly every situation, these notes enable you to use Microsoft Windows more confidently.

TASK

before

Maximize a window

Oops!
If the Exit Windows dialog box appears, you clicked on the Control menu box for the Program Manager. Click on Cancel.

1. Open the **Accessories** window.

   To open the window, point to the Accessories icon and double-click the left mouse button. For more information, see *TASK: Open a window.*

2. Point to the **Control menu box** and click the left mouse button.

   Remember that the Control menu box is the small bar in the title bar of the window. Clicking on this menu box displays the Control menu.

3. Point to **Maximize** and click the left mouse button.

   This step selects the Maximize command. The window fills the Program Manager screen. You see *Program Manager (Accessories)* in the title bar.

   Maximize, Minimize, and Restore are three separate functions. Maximize expands the window so that it fills the entire screen. Minimize returns the window to an icon. Restore returns the window to its last size and location.

52

Easy Windows

Before and After Illustrations

Each task includes Before and After illustrations that show how the computer screen will look before and after you follow the numbered steps in the Task section.

Review section

After you learn a procedure by following a specific example, you can refer to the Review section for a quick summary of the task. The Review section gives you the more generic steps for completing a task so that you can apply them to your own work. You can use these steps as a quick reference to refresh your memory about how to perform procedures.

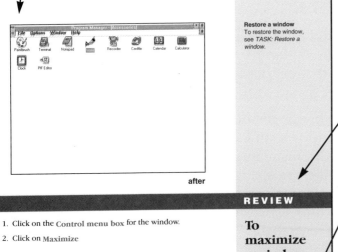

after

Restore a window
To restore the window, see *TASK: Restore a window.*

REVIEW

1. Click on the Control menu box for the window.
2. Click on Maximize

To maximize a window

Try a shortcut
To maximize a window quickly, click on the Maximize button. The Maximize button is an up arrow in the title bar of the window.

Other notes

The extra margin notes explain a little more about each procedure. These notes define terms, explain other options, and refer you to other sections, when applicable.

53

How To Follow an Exercise

Microsoft Windows is flexible because it enables you to perform a task many different ways. For consistency, this book makes certain assumptions about how your computer is set up and how you use Microsoft Windows. As you follow along with each exercise, keep these key points in mind:

- This book assumes that you have a hard drive and that you followed the basic program installation. This book assumes that you have installed a printer and that you have not changed any program defaults.

- This book assumes that you use the mouse to select windows and commands. Remember that you can also access commands and windows using the keyboard.

- This book shows the screens in color. Your screens may appear in black and white or in different colors.

- Only the Before and After screens are illustrated. Screens are not shown for every step within an exercise. Where necessary, the text discusses screen messages and how you should respond to them.

- Because you can change the desktop by arranging the icons, opening windows, and so on, the windows in the Before and After screens may appear in a different location or be a different size. Also, you may have different group windows (sets of programs) on-screen, depending on what programs you have installed and what changes you have made.

Where To Get More Help

This book does not cover every Microsoft Windows feature or every way to complete a task. This book is geared toward the beginning reader—a reader who wants just the basics. This reader isn't ready for advanced features such as running more than one program or customizing the desktop. This book covers just the most common, basic features.

As you become more comfortable, you may need a more complete reference book. Que offers several Microsoft Windows books to suit your needs:

Using Microsoft Windows 3, 2nd Edition

Windows 3 QuickStart

Windows 3 Quick Reference

Also of interest:

Que's Computer User's Dictionary, 2nd Edition

Introduction to Personal Computers

The Basics

Understanding Your Computer System

Using a Mouse

Using Your Keyboard

Understanding Key Terms

Understanding How Microsoft Windows Is Set Up

Understanding the Windows Desktop

Selecting a Menu Command

Arranging Your Desktop

Easy Windows

Understanding Your Computer System

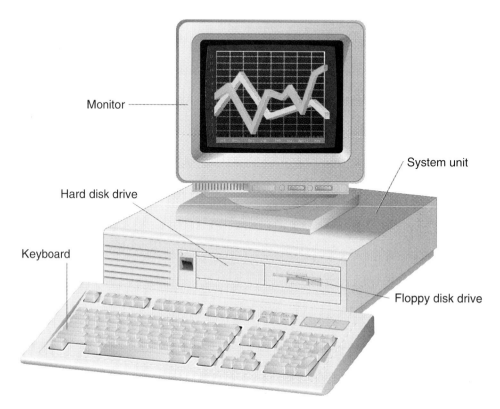

Monitor

System unit

Hard disk drive

Keyboard

Floppy disk drive

Your computer system is made up of these basic parts:

- The system unit
- The monitor
- The keyboard
- The floppy disk drive(s)
- The hard disk drive

You also may have a mouse and a printer.

System Unit. The system unit is the box that holds all the electrical components of your computer. The floppy disk drive and hard disk drive are also usually inside the system unit. (The size of the system unit varies.) Somewhere on this box, you find an On switch. To use your computer, you must flip it on.

Monitor. The monitor displays on-screen what you type on the keyboard. Your monitor may also have a separate On switch. Turn on this switch, also.

Keyboard. The keyboard enables you to communicate with the computer. You use it to type entries and to issue commands. You type on the keyboard just as you do on a regular typewriter. A keyboard also has special keys that you use. (Different computers have different keyboards.) These keys are discussed in the section Using Your Keyboard.

Floppy Disk Drive. The floppy disk drive is the door into your computer. It enables you to put information onto the computer and place it on the hard drive and to take information from the computer and place it on a floppy disk.

Hard Disk Drive. The hard disk drive stores the programs and files with which you work. To use Microsoft Windows, you must have a hard disk drive.

Printer. A printer gives you a paper copy of your on-screen work. To print, you need to attach and install a printer. Installing a printer tells Microsoft Windows what printer you have.

Mouse. A mouse is a pointing device that enables you to move the mouse pointer on-screen, to select windows, and to issue commands.

Using a Mouse

Using the mouse is the easiest and most natural way to learn Microsoft Windows and Microsoft Windows programs. This book assumes that you are using a mouse. (Using the keyboard is covered in the Guide to Basic Keyboard Operations in the Reference part.)

When you move the mouse on the desk, the mouse pointer moves on-screen. You can use the mouse to

- Open windows
- Close windows
- Open menus
- Select menu commands

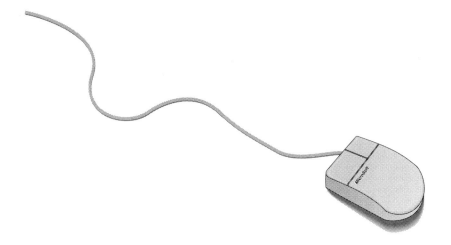

There are three types of mouse actions.

Action	Procedure
Click	Position the mouse pointer on an item, press the left mouse button, and then release the mouse button.
Double-click	Position the mouse pointer on an item and press the left mouse button twice in rapid succession.
Drag	Position the mouse pointer on an item. Press and hold the left mouse button and then move the mouse. When you are finished dragging, release the mouse button.

Keep these terms in mind as you follow a task.

If you double-click the mouse and nothing happens, you might not have clicked quickly enough. Try again.

Be sure to click the left mouse button. (You can change the mouse setup so that the right button works. See the Microsoft Windows manual or Using Microsoft Windows 3, 2nd Edition, for more information.)

Using Your Keyboard

A computer keyboard is just like a typewriter, only a keyboard has these additional keys:

- Function keys
- Arrow keys
- Other special keys (such as the Esc key)

These keys are located in different places on different keyboards. For example, sometimes the function keys are located across the top of the keyboard. Sometimes they are located on the left side of the keyboard.

The examples in this book are based on the Enhanced keyboard. Your keyboard has the same keys, but they may be in a different location. You can familiarize yourself with the keyboard by reading the names on the keys.

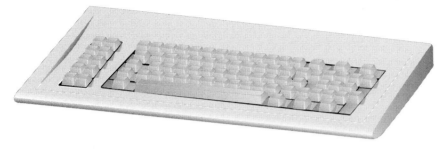

Original PC Keyboard

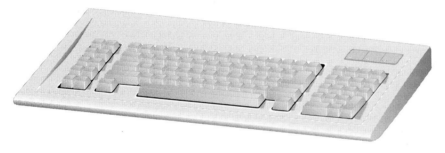

AT Keyboard

Enhanced Keyboard

Important Keys

Three important keys to remember are the

- F1 key
- Esc key
- Enter key

The F1 key is the Help key. Press this key to get on-line help about a particular feature. See TASK: Get help for complete information.

Esc is the Escape key. Press this key to escape or back out of a situation.

The Enter key is the same as the Return or carriage return key on a typewriter. When you are typing text, pressing Enter ends the line and moves the mouse pointer to the next line. When you are selecting a command, pressing Enter confirms the command. Sometimes the Enter key is called the Return key.

Troubleshooting List

You can use these troubleshooting tips when using Microsoft Windows:

- To back out of a menu, press the Esc key.
- If you see a dialog box and you don't know how to respond to it, press the Esc key.
- If you see an error message, press the Esc key to clear the message.
- If you cannot remember how to complete a particular task, press the F1 key and use the Help index to find and display on-screen help about a topic.

Understanding Key Terms

To use Microsoft Windows, you should understand the following key terms:

application.   A computer program that is used for a particular task, such as word processing. In most cases, *program* and *application* mean the same thing and can be used interchangeably.

dialog box.   An on-screen window that displays further command options. Many times, a dialog box reminds you of the consequences or results of a command and asks you to confirm that you want to proceed with the action.

directory.   A disk area that stores information about files. A directory is like a drawer in a file cabinet. Within that drawer, you can store several files.

DOS.   An acronym for Disk Operating System. DOS manages the details of your system, such as storing and retrieving programs and files.

file.   The various individual reports, memos, databases, and letters that you store on your hard drive (or floppy disk) for future use.

icon.   A small on-screen picture that represents a program group, a program, a document, or other elements within Microsoft Windows.

program group.   A collection of programs. These programs are stored in a window that contains program items. The group window is represented with an icon.

program item.   An icon for an application.

window.   A rectangular area on-screen that displays an application or a document. A window can contain an application, icons that represent an application, or a document that you have created in an application. Everything in Microsoft Windows is contained in a window.

Understanding How Microsoft Windows Is Set Up

Microsoft Windows is more than one program—it is several programs that work together. You should understand the relationship of some of these programs and program groups:

- Program Manager
- Main Program Group
- File Manager
- Accessories Program Group
- Games Program Group
- Microsoft Windows Applications Program Group
- Non-Microsoft Windows Applications Program Group

Program Manager

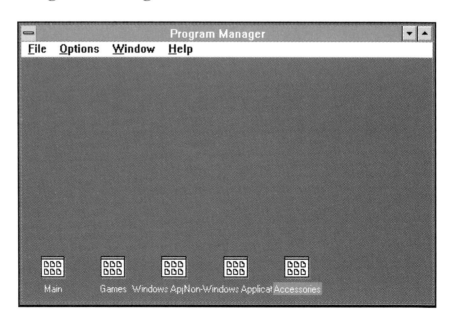

The Program Manager is the central Microsoft Windows program. When you start Microsoft Windows, the Program Manager starts automatically. When you exit Microsoft Windows, you exit the Program Manager. You cannot run Microsoft Windows if you are not running the Program Manager.

The Program Manager does what its name implies—it manages programs. You use it to organize applications into groups and to start programs.

Main Program Group

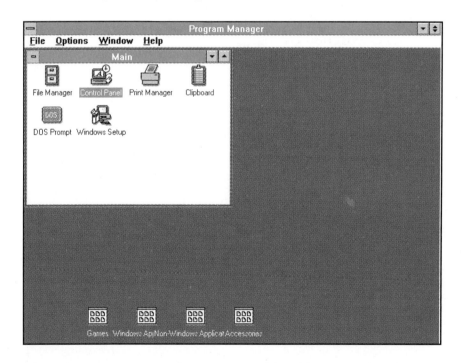

The Main Program Group is created by Microsoft Windows. Within this group, you find Microsoft Windows system applications, which are programs that help you work with your system (computer).

The Main Program Group includes the File Manager, Print Manager, DOS Prompt, Windows Setup, Control Panel, and Clipboard.

File Manager

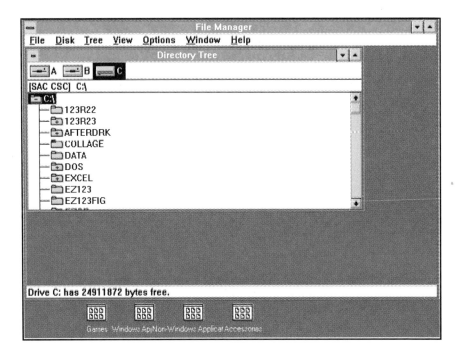

The File Manager program is provided with Microsoft Windows. This program is stored in the Main program Group and is used to manage files. The File Manager is covered in the File Manager section of the Task/Review part of this book.

Accessories Program Group

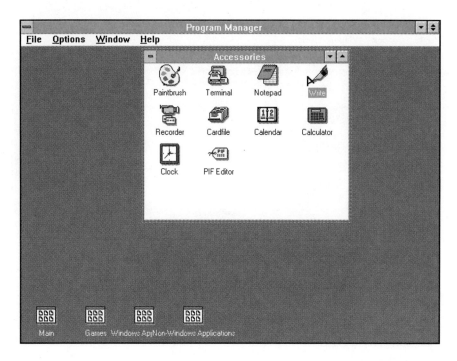

The Accessories program group is created by Microsoft Windows and contains accessory programs that are provided with Microsoft Windows. The following list includes some of these programs:

Program	Function
Calculator	Displays a calculator on-screen.
Clock	Displays the time on-screen.
Notepad	Enables you to enter, print, and edit notes.
Calendar	Enables you to enter and review appointments.
Cardfile	Enables you to enter, edit, sort, and delete cards, similar to a Rolodex card file.
Write	Enables you to create, edit, format, and print word processing documents.
Paintbrush	Enables you to create, edit, and print drawings. Paintbrush is a complete draw program.

The *Accessory Programs* section of the Task/Review part of this book covers basic tasks related to these programs.

Games Program Group

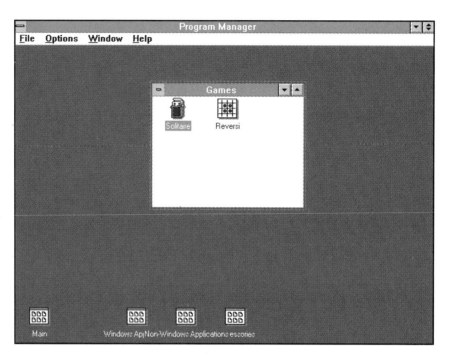

The Games program group contains two games: Solitaire and Reversi. For information on playing these games, see your Microsoft Windows manual or *Using Microsoft Windows 3,* 2nd Edition.

Windows Applications Group

When you install Microsoft Windows, the Setup program looks at the programs on your hard disk. If you have any Microsoft Windows programs (programs designed specifically to run under Microsoft Windows), Setup creates a program icon for them and stores them in a group named Windows Applications.

Non–Windows Applications Group

During setup, Microsoft Windows also finds any non-Windows programs (DOS-based programs) and creates a program group for these applications. These applications are stored in the Non-Windows Applications group.

Understanding the Windows Desktop

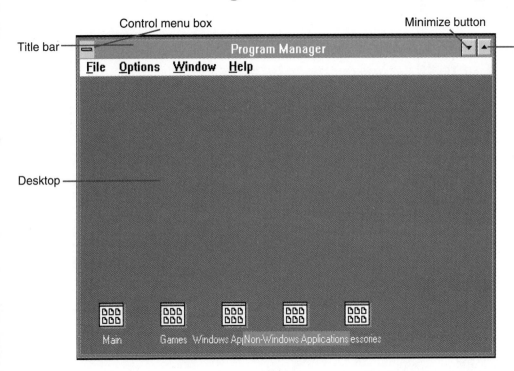

After you start Microsoft Windows, you see the desktop. (If you want to start the program and follow along, see *TASK: Start Microsoft Windows*. This is the first task in the Task/Review part.)

To use Microsoft Windows effectively, you should learn the different parts of the screen.

The desktop is the screen background on which windows and icons are displayed.

The title bar displays the name of the window.

The Control menu box enables you to manipulate windows. See *Controlling Microsoft Windows* later in this section.

The Maximize and Minimize buttons enable you to size windows. See *Maximizing and Minimizing Microsoft Windows* later in this section.

Controlling Microsoft Windows

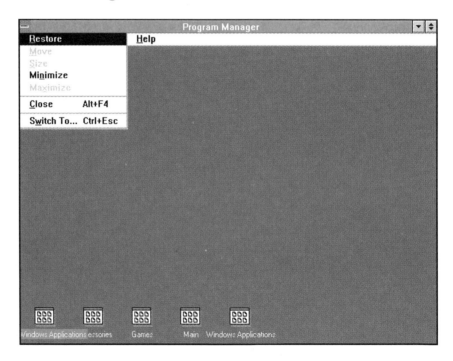

Most windows have a Control menu box in the upper left corner in the title bar. Clicking on this bar opens the Control menu. You use this menu to manipulate the window. Double-clicking the Control menu box closes the window.

Maximizing and Minimizing Microsoft Windows

The title bar contains a Maximize button and a Minimize button. Click on the Maximize button to expand the window so that it covers the entire desktop. Click on the Minimize button to restore the window to an icon. See *TASK: Minimize a window*, *TASK: Maximize a window*, and *TASK: Restore a window* for more information.

Scrolling a Window

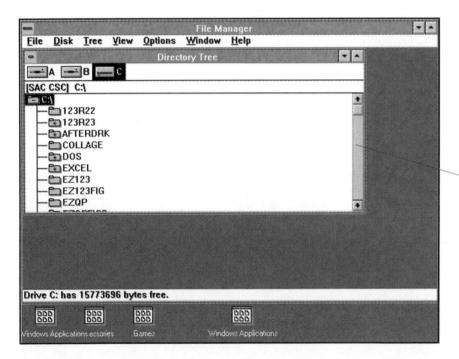

Scroll bar

Sometimes a window can display only part of its contents. For example, only the first part of a file list may appear in a window. To display the other contents, you scroll or move through the window.

Scroll bars appear at the bottom and right of a window. Most of the scroll bar is shaded. Inside the scroll bar is a scroll box that indicates the relative position of the window display. If the scroll box is in the center, for example, you are viewing the center of the window. At the ends of the bars are scroll arrows.

You can use two methods to scroll the window:

- Click on the scroll arrow to scroll the window in the direction of the arrow one line at a time.

- Drag the darker area of the scroll bar to move the relative distance in that direction.

Selecting a Menu Command

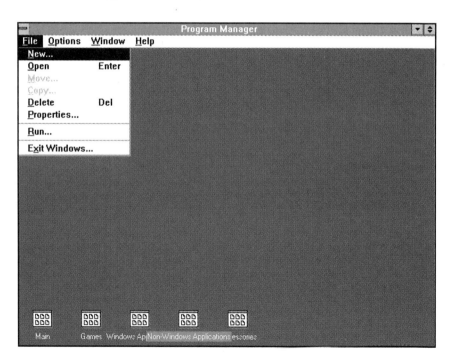

The menu bar contains the names of the menus. To open a menu, click on the name in the menu bar. For example, you can click on File.

To select a menu command, click on that command. To select the Open command, for example, click on Open.

When a command is followed by an ellipsis (...), you must specify additional options before you can initiate the command. When you select the command, a dialog box appears. The dialog box may ask you to enter text, make a choice about options, or confirm an operation. When you select the File Open command, for example, you see the File Open dialog box.

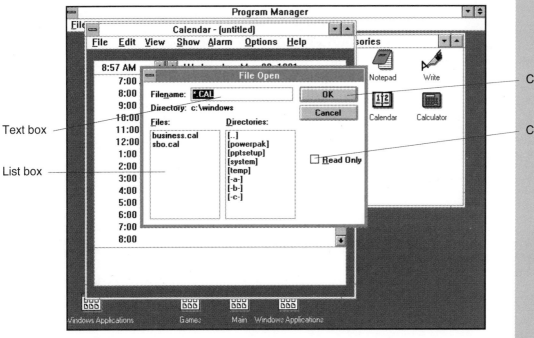

Dialog boxes can contain different elements. Each item may require a different type of selection process. You should be familiar with the following elements:

check box. A square box that appears in a dialog box. Check boxes can be checked (selected) or unchecked (unselected). To select a check box, click in the box. To unselect a check box, click again in that box.

command button. A choice of action that is displayed in a dialog box. Two common command buttons are OK and Cancel. To select a command button, click on it. Most dialog boxes have a "default" command button. To select this button, you can also press Enter.

drop-down list box. A box that lists the default choice. Other choices are available. To display the other choices, click the arrow in the square box at the right.

list box. A list of available choices—such as file names. To select an item in a list, click on it. Sometimes list boxes have scroll bars that you can use to scroll through the list.

option button. A round button that appears in a dialog box. To select an option, click in the Option button. A dot appears in the button. You cannot activate more than one option button at a time.

text box. A box within a dialog box in which you type information—such as a file name. To select a text box, click in the box. (Sometimes the mouse pointer is already in the text box.)

Arranging Your Desktop

When you work with many different windows, your desktop can become confusing. Remember that Microsoft Windows is supposed to simplify your work. To keep things simple, you can rearrange your desktop. The next time you start Microsoft Windows, it remembers this arrangement and displays the same layout on-screen. (You must make sure that the Save Changes check box is selected when you quit).

Keep in mind these key points:

When you minimize a program, it is still running in memory. A program icon does appear on-screen. If the Program Manager is displayed full-size, however, you cannot see the icon. Be sure that you exit all programs properly.

The Program Manager is like any other window—it can be moved, sized, minimized, and maximized. This capability can be confusing if you accidentally minimize the Program Manager and it disappears. Remember that the Program Manager is minimized to an icon; to restore it, simply double-click on the icon.

When you quit, Microsoft Windows remembers the arrangement of windows. Applications do not, however, reopen to where they were when you quit Microsoft Windows.

For information on manipulating windows, see these tasks:

TASK: Open a window

TASK: Close a window

TASK: Select a window

TASK: Maximize a window

TASK: Restore a window

TASK: Minimize a window

TASK: Move a window

TASK: Resize a window

Task/Review

Program Manager

File Manager

Accessory Programs

Easy Windows

Program Manager

This section covers the following tasks:

Start Microsoft Windows

Exit Microsoft Windows

Get help

Open a window

Close a window

Change a program group name

Select a window

Maximize a window

Restore a window

Minimize a window

Move a window

Resize a window

Arrange windows

Move an icon

Arrange icons

Start Microsoft Windows

before

`C:\>`

Oops!
If the program doesn't start, be sure that you specified the correct directory. If you installed the program in a different directory, type this directory for step 4.

1. **Turn on the computer and monitor.**

   Every computer has a different location for its On/Off switch. Check the side, the front, and the back of your computer. Your monitor also may have a separate On switch; if so, you also need to turn on the monitor.

2. **If necessary, respond to the prompts for date and time.**

   When you first turn on the computer, some systems ask you to enter the current date and time. (Many of the newer models enter the time and date automatically. If you are not prompted for these entries, don't worry.)

   If you are prompted, type the current date and press Enter. Then type the current time and press Enter. Your computer keeps track of the date and time when you save files to disk. Therefore, entering the date and time ensures that your file information is complete.

3. **Make sure that you have installed the program.**

   To use Microsoft Windows, it must be installed. You need to install the program only once. Follow the installation procedures outlined in the Microsoft Windows manual that came with the software. This book assumes that the program is installed in the \WINDOWS directory on drive C.

4. **Type cd\windows.**

   Typing *cd\windows* tells the computer to change to the Microsoft Windows directory. This directory is named windows and contains the Microsoft Windows program files. These files are needed to start and run the program.

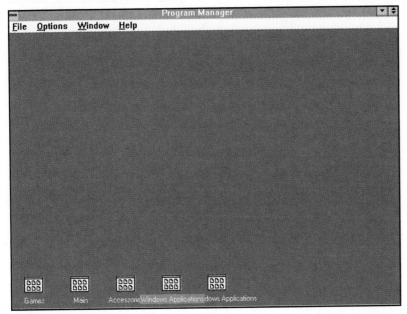

after

What is an icon?
An icon is a picture that represents a group window, an application, a document, or other elements within Microsoft Windows.

What is a window?
A window is a rectangular area on-screen in which you view an application or a document icon.

5. **Press Enter.**

   Pressing Enter places you in the Microsoft Windows directory. You see the prompt C:\WINDOWS>.

6. **Type win.**

   Win is the command that starts the program.

7. **Press Enter.**

   Pressing Enter confirms that you want to start Microsoft Windows. The Program Manager appears in a window on-screen. The Program Manager is an application that comes with Microsoft Windows.

   The Program Manager window includes many different elements, such as the menu bar, title bar, icons, and so on. See the preceding part, The Basics, for a description of each of these elements.

REVIEW

1. Turn on your computer and monitor.

2. Respond to the prompts for date and time, if necessary.

3. Make sure that you have installed the program.

4. Type **cd\windows** and press **Enter**.

5. Type **win** and press **Enter**.

To start Microsoft Windows

before

Exit Microsoft Windows

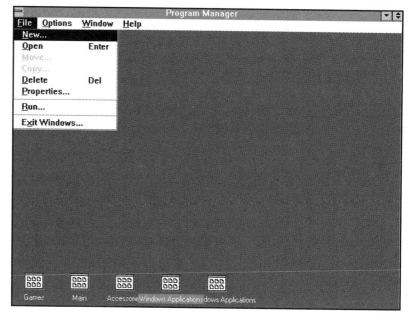

Oops!
If you do not want to quit, click Cancel in the Exit Windows dialog box.

1. Point to **File** in the menu bar and click the left mouse button.

   This step opens the File menu. You see a list of File commands. The last command is Exit Windows.

2. Point to **Exit Windows** and click the left mouse button.

   This step tells Microsoft Windows that you want to exit. The Exit Windows dialog box appears. This box reminds you that you are exiting the program.

   Notice that this dialog box also includes the prompt Save Changes. The prompt has a box with a check mark next to it. This means that Microsoft Windows will remember all the settings it used for the current work session, such as open windows, arrangement of windows, and other options.

3. Point to **OK** and click the left mouse button.

   This step confirms that you do want to exit. You return to DOS.

c:\>

after

**Restart Microsoft
Windows**
To restart Microsoft
Windows, see *TASK:
Start Microsoft Windows.*

1. Click on **File** in the menu bar.

2. Click on the **Exit** command.

3. Click on **OK** or press **Enter**.

To exit Microsoft Windows

Try a shortcut
As a shortcut for steps 1
and 2, double-click on the
Control menu box.

Get help

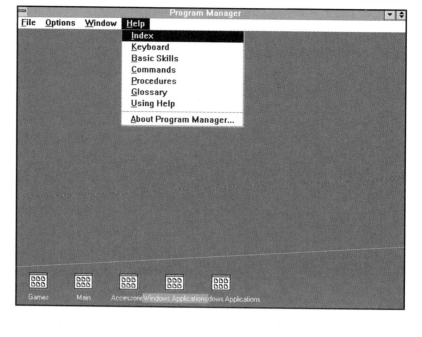

before

Oops!
To close the Help window, point to the Control menu box and double-click the mouse button.

1. **Point to Help in the menu bar and click the left mouse button.**

   This step opens the Help menu. On-screen, you see a list of Help menu options—Index, Keyboard, Basic Skills, and so on.

2. **Point to Index and click the left mouse button.**

   This step selects the Index command. The Help window for the Program Manager opens. You see the name of the help window in the title bar.

   A description of how to use the Index appears in the window. You can select between two other indexes: Program Manager Help Index and Windows Help Index.

   Microsoft Windows offers many ways to get help, and the Help feature has its own menu system. For complete information on all Help options, see your Microsoft Windows manual or *Using Microsoft Windows 3*, 2nd Edition.

3. **Point to the Program Manager Help Index and click the left mouse button.**

   The Program Manager Help Index category is listed in the window—not on the menu bar. This step selects the Program Manager Help Index and displays a list of categories and topics. When the mouse pointer is on a topic for which you can get help, it changes to a hand with pointing finger.

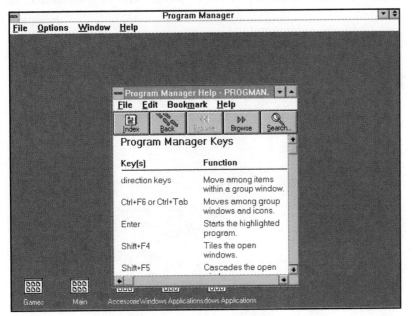

after

Scroll the Help screen
To scroll through the Help screen, click on the scroll arrow on the right side of the screen. See The Basics part for information on scrolling a window.

4. Point to the topic **Program Manager Keys** and click the left mouse button.

   The topic Program Manager Keys is under the heading Keyboard.

   This step selects the topic Program Manager Keys and displays a list of keys that you can use in the Program Manager.

Try a shortcut
As a shortcut for steps 1 and 2, press the F1 key.

5. Point to the **Control menu box** and click the left mouse button.

   The Control menu box is the small bar to the left of the window's title bar. Clicking on this menu box displays the Control menu.

6. Point to **Close** and click the left mouse button.

   This step selects the Close command, which closes the Help window.

REVIEW

To get help

1. Click on **Help** in the menu bar.

2. Click on the **Index** command.

3. Click on the index that you want.

4. Click on the topic that you want.

5. Click on the **Control menu box** when you want to close the Help window.

6. Click on **Close**.

Open a window

before

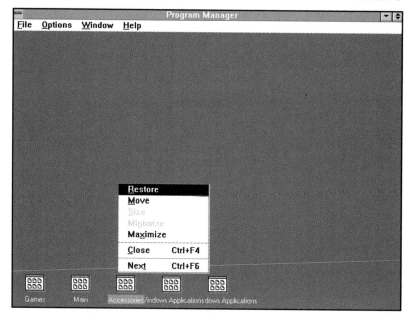

Oops!
To close the window, see
TASK: Close a window.

1. **Point to the Accessories icon and click the left mouse button.**

   All programs are stored in group windows. A group window is indicated by a group icon. The name of the group window appears under the group icon and is highlighted when you click on the icon.

   This step opens the Control menu for this window. You use this menu to manipulate the program window (restore, move, size, close, and so on).

2. **Point to Restore and click the left mouse button.**

   This step tells Microsoft Windows to restore (or open) the group window. The Accessories window appears. You see various accessory programs, such as Calculator, Calendar, and so on. These programs are provided with Microsoft Windows and are described later in this book.

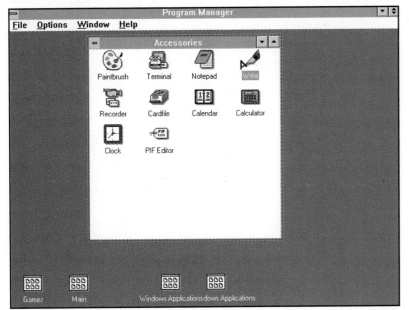

after

Window looks different?
Do not worry if your screen is different from the After screen. Your desktop may be organized differently. You can still perform all the tasks.

1. Point to the window icon and click the left mouse button.

2. Click on **Restore**.

To open a window

Try a shortcut
To open a window quickly, point to the icon and click the mouse twice in rapid succession. Clicking twice is called double-clicking.

Close a window

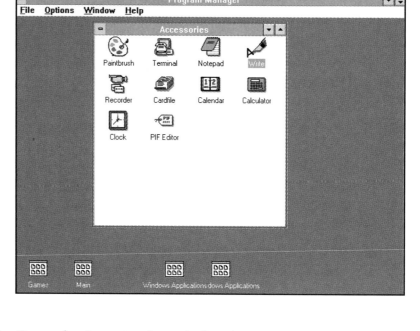

Oops!
If the Exit Windows dialog box appears, you clicked on the Control menu box for the Program Manager and not for the window you want to close. Click on Cancel.

1. **Open the Accessories window.**

   To open the window, point to the Accessories icon and double-click the left mouse button. (Double-click means to press the mouse button twice in rapid succession.) For more information, see *TASK: Open a window*.

2. **Point to the Control menu box and click the left mouse button.**

   Remember that the Control menu box is the small bar to the left of the window's title bar. Clicking on this box displays the Control menu.

3. **Point to Close and click the left mouse button.**

   This step selects the Close command. The window closes and is restored to an icon.

   Your desktop can get confusing with different windows open in different sizes. Try closing all windows and then opening just those that you need.

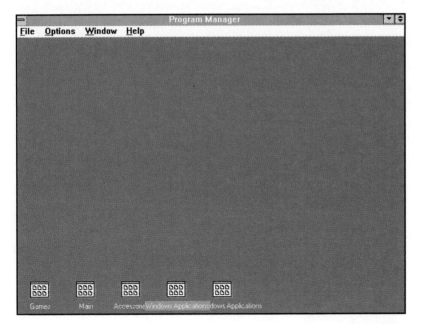

REVIEW

1. Click on the **Control menu box**.

2. Click on **Close**.

To close a window

Change a program group name

before

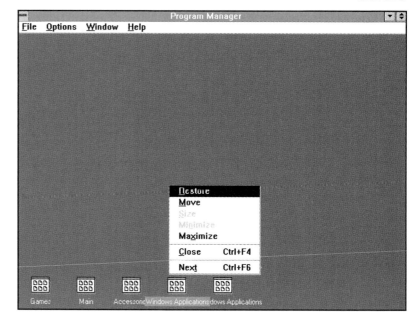

1. **Point to the Windows Applications icon and click the left mouse button.**

   This step selects the Windows Applications program group. The Control menu for this window appears.

   When you install Microsoft Windows, five program groups are created: Accessories, Main, Games, Windows Applications, and Non-Windows Applications. (See the part, The Basics, for more information on program groups.) The default names for each of the program names overlap when the icons are arranged along the bottom of the screen. You can move the icons to allow for more room (see *TASK: Move an icon*), but the next time you start Microsoft Windows, the icons are arranged along the bottom again.

   So that the names don't overlap, shorten the names.

2. **Point to File in the menu bar and click the left mouse button.**

   This steps opens the File menu.

3. **Point to Properties and click the left mouse button.**

   This step selects the Properties command. You see the Program Group Properties dialog box. Inside this box, you see two text boxes: Description and Group File. The Description text box contains the current program group name. (The mouse pointer is positioned inside this box.)

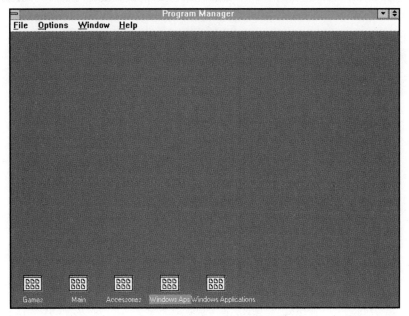

after

4. Type **Windows Aps**.

   Windows Aps is a shortened version of *Windows Applications*. You can name the program group with a different name.

5. Press **Enter**.

   Pressing Enter confirms the new name. The new name appears below the icon in the Program Manager window.

   Follow this same procedure to change *Non-Windows Applications* to *DOS Aps*. The screens in this book show the icons with these names. Your icons will display the names that you assign to them.

Customize Microsoft Windows
You can create other program groups and move programs from one group to another. For complete information, see *Using Microsoft Windows 3,* 2nd Edition.

R E V I E W

1. Select the group icon that you want to change.

2. Click on **File** in the menu bar.

3. Click on the **Properties** command.

4. In the Description text box, type the new name.

5. Press **Enter**.

To change a program group name

Select a window

before

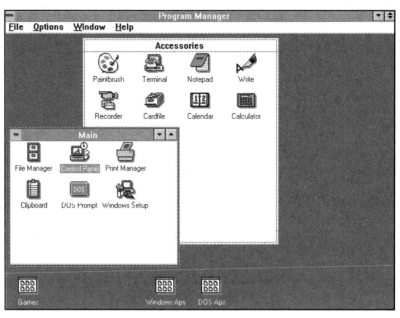

Oops!
To change back to the window that was active, follow this same procedure.

1. **Open the Accessories window.**

   To open the window, point to the Accessories icon and double-click the left mouse button. For more information, see *TASK: Open a window*.

2. **Open the Main window.**

   To open this window, point to the Main icon and double-click the left mouse button. For more information, see *TASK: Open a window*.

   You now have two windows open on-screen. The window that you just opened is the current or active window. Notice that the border and title bar of the active window are colored or shaded differently from those of the other open windows. (The title bar is the top line of the window and includes the name of the window. The border is the edge of the window.)

3. **Point to Window in the menu bar and click the left mouse button.**

   This step opens the Windows menu. You see a list of numbered windows. The current window (Main) has a check mark next to it.

4. **Point to the Accessories window name and click the left mouse button.**

   This step selects the Accessories window. This window moves to the top of the desktop and is the active window. The border and title bar appear in a different color or shade.

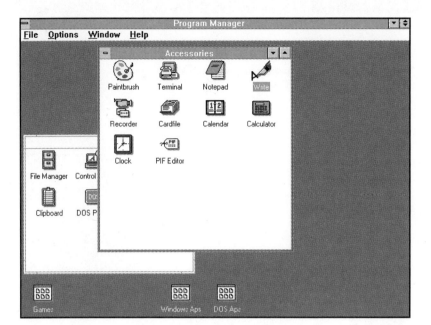

after

Switch programs
Use this procedure to
switch among windows in
the Program Manager.
See *TASK: Switch to a
different program.*

1. Click on Window in the menu bar.

2. From the list, click on the name of the window that you
   want to make active.

To select a window

Try a shortcut
If you can see the window
that you want on-screen,
you can click anywhere
on that window to
select it.

Maximize
a window

before

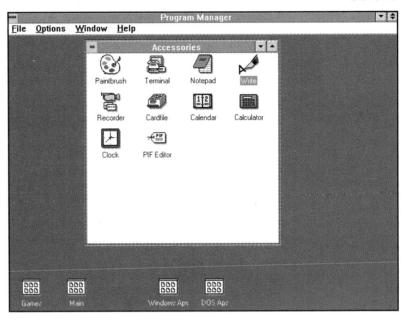

Oops!
If the Exit Windows dialog
box appears, you clicked
on the Control menu box
for the Program Manager.
Click on Cancel.

1. **Open the Accessories window.**

   To open the window, point to the Accessories icon and double-click the left mouse button. For more information, see *TASK: Open a window*.

2. **Point to the Control menu box and click the left mouse button.**

   Remember that the Control menu box is the small bar in the title bar of the window. Clicking on this menu box displays the Control menu.

3. **Point to Maximize and click the left mouse button.**

   This step selects the Maximize command. The window fills the Program Manager screen. You see `Program Manager- (Accessories)` in the title bar.

   Maximize, Minimize, and Restore are three separate functions. Maximize expands the window so that it fills the entire screen. Minimize returns the window to an icon. Restore returns the window to its last size and location.

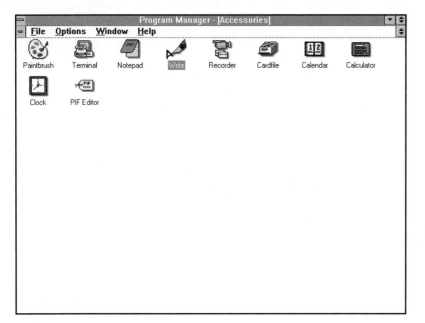

after

Restore a window
To restore the window,
see *TASK: Restore a
window.*

REVIEW

1. Click on the **Control menu box** for the window.

2. Click on **Maximize**.

To maximize a window

Try a shortcut
To maximize a window
quickly, click on the
Maximize button. The
Maximize button is an up
arrow in the title bar of the
window.

Restore a window

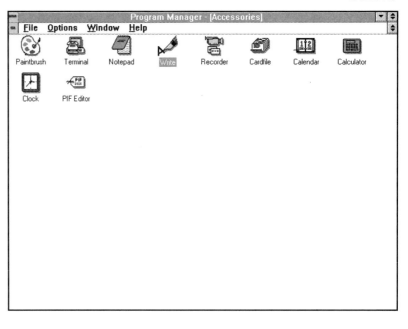

Oops!
If the Exit Windows dialog box appears, you clicked on the Control menu box for the Program Manager. Click on Cancel.

1. **Open the Accessories window.**

   To open the window, point to the Accessories icon and double-click the left mouse button. For more information, see *TASK: Open a window.*

   You use Restore after you have maximized or minimized the window. For this example, you want to maximize the window.

2. **Point to the Control menu box and click the left mouse button.**

   Remember that the Control menu box is the small bar in the title bar of the window. Clicking on this menu box displays the Control menu.

3. **Point to Maximize and click the left mouse button.**

   This step selects the Maximize command. The window expands to fill the Program Manager screen. Now that the window is maximized, you can restore it to its original size.

4. **Point to the Control menu box and click the left mouse button.**

   This step opens the Control menu.

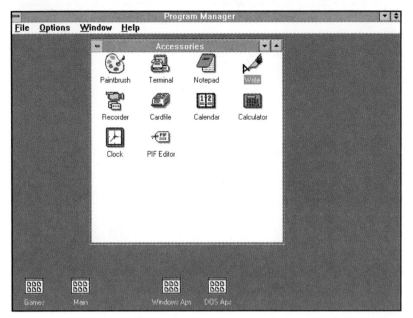

after

5. Point to **Restore** and click the left mouse button.

   This step selects the Restore command. The window is restored to its original size and location.

   Maximize, Minimize, and Restore are three separate functions. Maximize expands the window so that it fills the entire screen. Minimize returns the window to an icon. Restore returns the window to its last size and location.

1. Maximize or minimize the window.

2. Click on the **Control menu box**.

3. Click on the **Restore** command.

To restore a window

Remember...
You cannot restore a window unless it has been maximized or minimized.

Try a shortcut
To restore a window quickly, click on the Restore button. The Restore button is a two-headed (up and down) arrow in the title bar.

Minimize a window

before

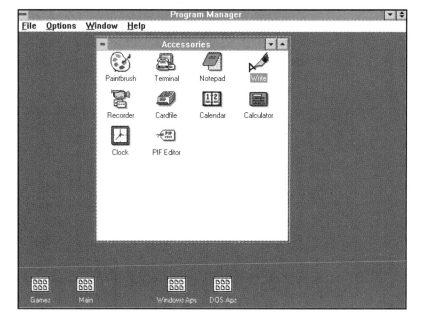

Oops!
If the Exit Windows dialog box appears, you clicked on the Control menu box for the Program Manager. Click on Cancel.

1. **Open the Accessories window.**

   To open the window, point to the Accessories icon and double-click the left mouse button. For more information on this step, see *TASK: Open a window.*

2. **Point to the Control menu box and click the left mouse button.**

   Remember that the Control menu box is the small bar in the title bar. Clicking on this menu box displays the Control menu.

3. **Point to Minimize and click the left mouse button.**

   This step selects the Minimize command. The window is restored to an icon.

   Maximize, Minimize, and Restore are three separate functions. Maximize expands the window so that it fills the entire screen. Minimize returns the window to an icon. Restore returns the window to its last size and location.

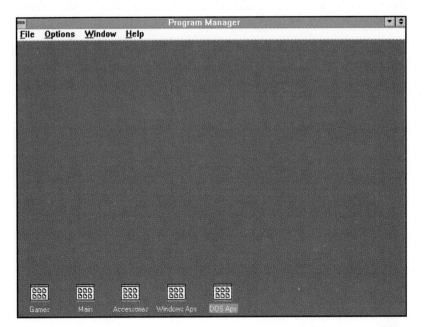

after

1. Click on the **Control menu box** of the window that you want to minimize.

2. Click on **Minimize**.

To minimize a window

Try a shortcut
To minimize a window quickly, click on the Minimize button. The Minimize button is a down arrow in the title bar.

Program Manager

Move a window

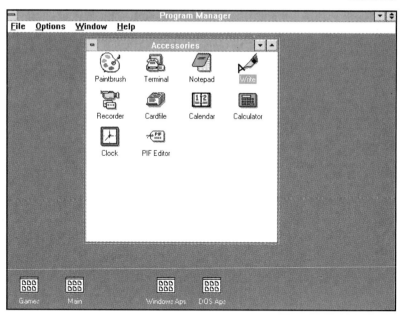

Oops!
If the window does not move, you may not have placed the mouse pointer on the title bar of the window. Reposition the mouse pointer correctly and try again.

1. **Open the Accessories window.**

   To open the window, point to the Accessories icon and double-click the left mouse button. For more information, see *TASK: Open a window*.

2. **Point to the title bar.**

   This step selects the window that you want to move. Be sure that you point to the title bar and not to the window border. The title bar displays the window name. Pointing to the window border resizes the window rather than moves it.

3. **Press and hold the mouse button.**

   This step prepares the window to be moved. Notice that the border turns a lighter shade.

4. **Drag the mouse up and to the right until the window is in the upper right corner.**

   Dragging the mouse lets you reposition the window. As you drag, you see the outline of the window.

5. **Release the mouse button.**

   Releasing the mouse button moves the window to the new location.

   If you have a lot of open windows and want to see them all, use the Arrange command. This command automatically sizes and moves windows so that all are displayed. See *TASK: Arrange windows*.

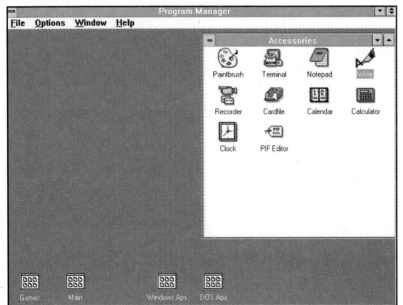

after

REVIEW

1. Open the window that you want to move. If the window is open, select the window. See *TASK: Open a window* and *TASK: Select a window*.

2. Point to the title bar.

3. Press and hold the mouse button and drag the window to the new location.

4. Release the mouse button.

To move a window

Resize a window

before

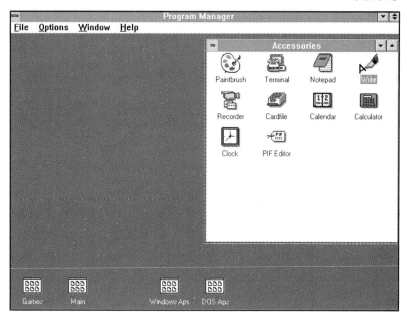

1. **Open the Accessories window.**

   To open the window, point to the Accessories icon and double-click the left mouse button. For more information, see *TASK: Open a window.*

2. **Position the mouse pointer on the left border.**

   This step selects the window border that you want to resize. You must position the mouse pointer exactly on the border. When the pointer is in the correct spot, it changes to a two-headed arrow.

3. **Press and hold the mouse button.**

   This step prepares the border to be resized. Notice that the border turns a lighter shade.

4. **Drag the mouse to the left until the window stretches to the left edge of the screen.**

   Dragging the mouse lets you resize the window. As you drag, you see the outline of the border.

5. **Release the mouse button.**

   Releasing the mouse button resizes the window.

   If you exit the program with windows open, Microsoft Windows remembers the size and arrangement of windows in the Program Manager.

   If you have a lot of open windows and want to see them all, use the Arrange command. This command automatically sizes and moves windows so that all are displayed. See *TASK: Arrange windows.*

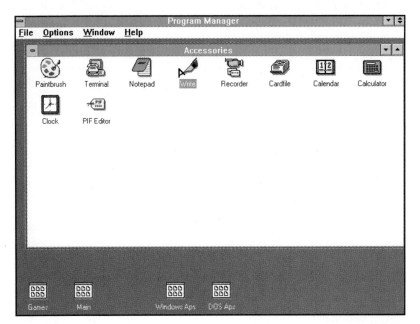

after

Resize other sides
You can resize the
window from the left,
right, top, or bottom by
pointing to the side that
you want to resize.

1. Open the window that you want to resize. If the window is open, select the window. See *TASK: Open a window* and *TASK: Select a window*.

2. Position the mouse pointer on the border that you want to move.

3. Press and hold the mouse button and drag the border to the new location.

4. Release the mouse button.

To resize a window

Arrange windows

before

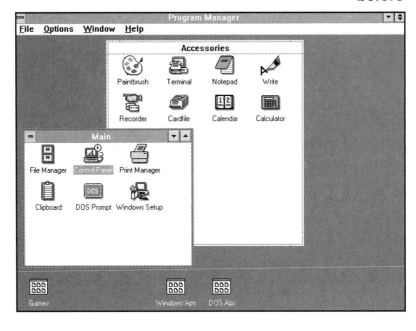

Oops!
If you don't like the arrangement, move, resize, or close the windows.

1. **Open the Accessories window.**

   To open the window, point to the Accessories icon and double-click the left mouse button. For more information, see *TASK: Open a window*.

2. **Open the Main window.**

   To open this window, point to the Main icon and double-click the left mouse button.

   You now have two windows open on-screen. The window that you just opened is the current or active window. Notice that the border and title bar of the active window are colored or shaded differently from the other open window.

3. **Point to the Window menu and click the left mouse button.**

   This step opens the Windows menu.

4. **Point to Tile and click the left mouse button.**

   This step selects the Tile command. The windows appear on-screen side-by-side. The icons appear at the bottom.

   If you have more than two windows, the windows are arranged so that you see them all.

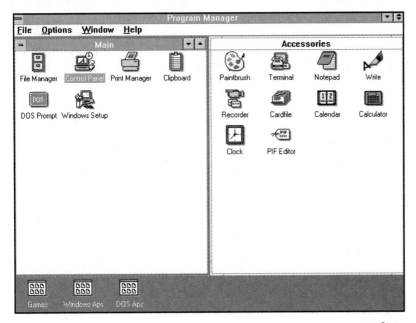

after

1. Open the windows that you want to arrange.

2. Click on the Window menu.

3. Click on the Tile command.

To arrange windows

Move an icon

Oops!
To return the icon to its original location, follow this same procedure. Or use the Arrange command; see *TASK: Arrange icons.*

before

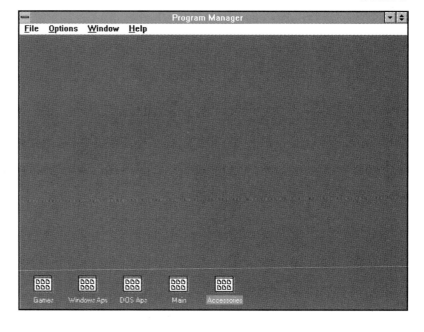

1. **Close all windows so that you only see the icons.**

   For information on closing a window, see *TASK: Close a window.*

2. **Point to the Accessories icon.**

   You want to move the Accessories icon.

   When you start Microsoft Windows, all the icons are aligned at the bottom of the window. You can move the icons on the desktop.

3. **Press and hold the mouse button.**

   This step selects the Accessories icon.

4. **Drag the Accessories icon to the upper left corner of the screen.**

   This step moves the Accessories icon to its new location.

5. **Release the mouse button.**

   Releasing the mouse button positions the Accessories icon in the new location.

   Notice that Microsoft Windows does not remember the position of your icons when you exit and restart the program. The icons always align along the bottom of the window.

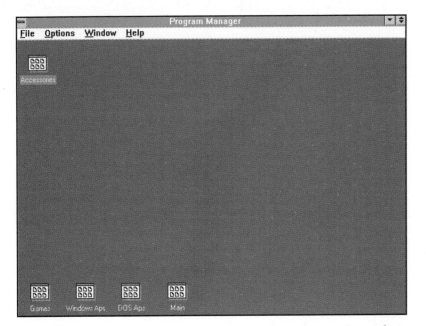

after

Remedy long icon names
Long icon names may overlap on-screen. You can move the icons, or you can shorten the icon names. See *TASK: Change a program group name.*

REVIEW

1. Point to the icon that you want to move.

2. Press and hold the mouse button.

3. Drag the icon to the new location.

4. Release the mouse button.

To move an icon

Arrange
icons

before

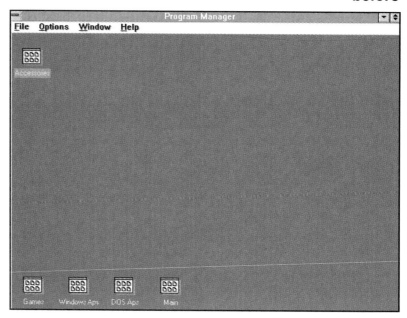

1. Close all windows so that you see only the group icons.

   For information on closing a window, see *TASK: Close a window.*

2. Move the **Accessories** icon to the upper left corner.

   To move the icon, press and hold the mouse button and then drag the icon to the upper left corner.

   For more information on moving an icon, see *TASK: Move an icon.*

3. Point to the **Window** menu and click the left mouse button.

   This step opens the Window menu.

4. Point to **Arrange Icons** and click the left mouse button.

   This step selects the Arrange icons command. The icons are arranged at the bottom of the window.

   Notice that Microsoft Windows does not remember the position of your icons when you exit and restart the program. The icons are always aligned along the bottom of the window.

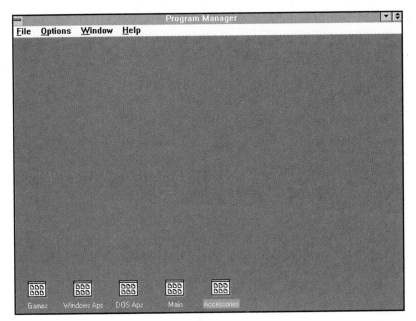

after

Arrange program icons
You can use this same procedure to arrange the program icons within a group window.

REVIEW

1. Click on the **Window** menu.

2. Click on the **Arrange Icons** command.

To arrange icons

File Manager

This section covers the following tasks:

Open the File Manager

Expand directories

Collapse directories

Select a drive

Display files

Display selected files

Select a file

Select multiple files

Copy a file

Delete a file

Rename a file

Move a file

Search for a file

Create a directory

Remove a directory

Close the File Manager

Open the File Manager

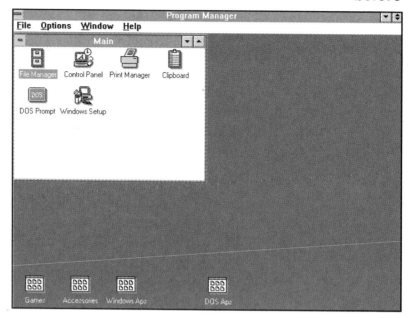

Oops!
To close the File Manager, double-click on the Control menu box next to the File Manager title bar. When the Exit File Manager dialog box appears, click on OK.

1. **Point to the Main group icon and double-click the mouse button.**

   This step opens the Main window. Double-click means to click the mouse button twice in rapid succession. This window stores programs—including the File Manager.

   You see icons for various programs: File Manager, Control Panel, Clipboard, and so on. These programs are provided with Windows.

2. **Point to the File Manager icon and double-click the mouse button.**

   The File Manager icon looks like a file drawer. This step opens the File Manager window. The title bar for this window appears at the top of the screen. The menu bar for the File Manager appears under the title bar.

   Within the File Manager window, you see a Directory Tree window. This window also has a title bar. Below the title bar, you see icons for each of your computer's drives. The current directory appears below the drive icons.

   In the Directory Tree Window, you see icons that look like folders. Each folder represents a directory. These are directory icons. The directories are listed in alphabetical order.

   Next to the directory icon you see the directory name. Your computer screen will look different from the example screens because your hard drive will have different directories.

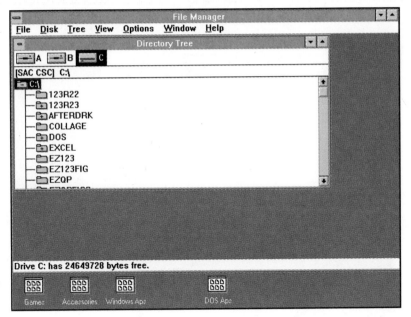

after

Notice that some directory icons have a + (plus sign) on them. This indicates that these directories contain other directories.

You can expand and collapse the directories that appear. You also can manipulate the Directory Tree window (move it, size it, maximize it, and so on), but you cannot close it without closing the File Manager.

REVIEW

1. Double-click on the **Main** group icon.

2. Double-click on the **File Manager** icon.

To open the File Manager

What is a directory?
A directory is a place on the computer where you store files, much like a drawer in a filing cabinet. A directory can contain files or other directories.

Remember...
Although the Directory Tree Window has a Control menu box, you cannot close this window. It is always open when the File Manager is open.

Expand directories

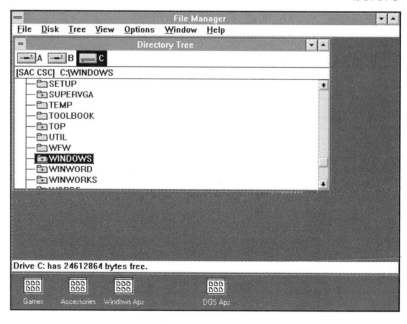

Oops!
If additional directories do not appear, the directory may not contain other directories or you may have clicked on the directory name, not the icon.

1. **Open the File Manager.**

   To open the File Manager, double-click on the Main group icon. Then double-click on the File Manager icon. For more information on this step, see *TASK: Open the File Manager*.

   The Directory Tree window appears. This window lists the directories in the root (or main) directory of drive C.

2. **Click on the down scroll arrow until you see the directory called WINDOWS.**

   This step enables you to see additional directories in the root directory of drive C. The down scroll arrow is located on the right side of the window. See The Basics part for information on scrolling a window.

   Notice that this directory icon is marked with a plus sign (+), which indicates that it contains other directories. The Before screen shows this step.

3. **Click on the WINDOWS directory icon.**

   This step expands the WINDOWS directory. Make sure that you click on the directory icon and not the directory name. You see the directories that are contained within this directory. You may have to scroll the window to see all the directories.

   The directory icon is marked with a minus sign (–) now. This reminds you that you can collapse the directory. See *TASK: Collapse directories* for more information.

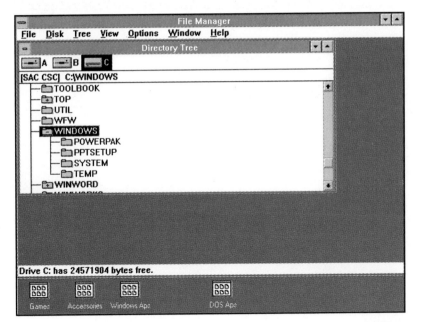

after

What is a root directory?
The root directory is the main directory. All other directories branch off from this main directory.

1. Open the **File Manager**.

2. Point to the icon of the directory that you want to expand.

3. Click the mouse button.

To expand directories

Collapse a directory
To collapse a directory, see *TASK: Collapse directories.*

Collapse directories

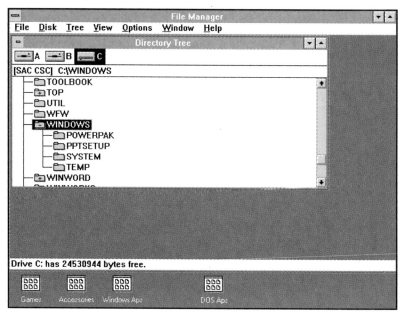

Oops!
Remember that you can only collapse directories that are expanded and that contain other directories.

1. Open the **File Manager**.

To open the File Manager, double-click on the Main group icon. Then double-click on the File Manager icon. For more information on this step, see *TASK: Open the File Manager*.

The Directory Tree window appears. This window lists the directories in the root (or main) directory of drive C.

2. Expand the WINDOWS directory.

You may have to scroll through the window to find the WINDOWS directory. The scroll arrows appear on the right side of the window. To scroll, click on the scroll arrow that points in the direction that you want to scroll. To scroll up, for example, click on the up scroll arrow.

To collapse a directory, it must be expanded first. To expand the directory, click on the directory icon. The directory now displays a minus sign (–), which reminds you that you can collapse the directory. The directories within this directory appear under the WINDOWS directory name. (The Before screen shows this step.)

3. Click on the **WINDOWS** directory icon.

This step collapses the directory. Be sure that you click on the directory icon and not the directory name.

Easy **Windows**

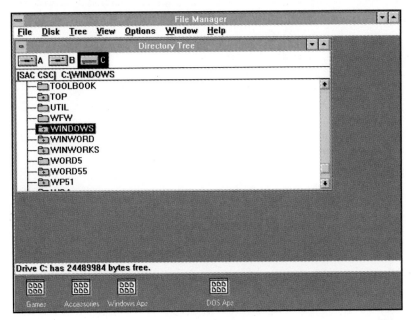

after

1. Open the **File Manager**.

2. Point to the icon of the directory that you want to collapse. Remember that you can collapse only expanded directories.

3. Click the mouse button.

To collapse directories

Select a drive

before

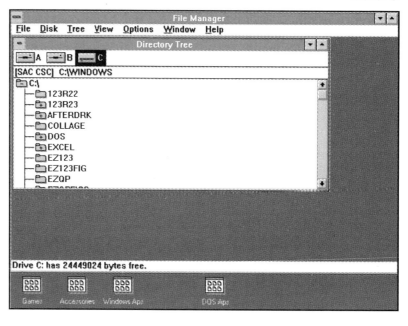

Oops!

If you see the message
`Cannot read from drive A:`, you didn't insert a diskette into the drive or you didn't close the drive door. Click on Cancel and begin again.

1. **Open the File Manager.**

   To open the File Manager, double-click on the Main group icon. Then double-click on the File Manager icon. For more information on this step, see *TASK: Open the File Manager*.

   The Directory Tree window appears. This window lists the directories in the root (or main) directory of drive C.

2. **Insert a floppy disk into floppy drive A.**

   You are inserting the diskette that you want to use. Every computer has at least one floppy drive, which is called drive A. You also may have additional floppy drives. Be sure that you close the drive door after you insert the diskette into the drive. If the door isn't closed, the computer cannot read the information on the diskette.

3. **Click on the drive A icon.**

   This step selects drive A and displays the folders (or directories) on this drive. If the disk does not contain any directories, you only see `A:\` next to a directory icon. To view the contents of this disk, double-click on the directory icon for A:\.

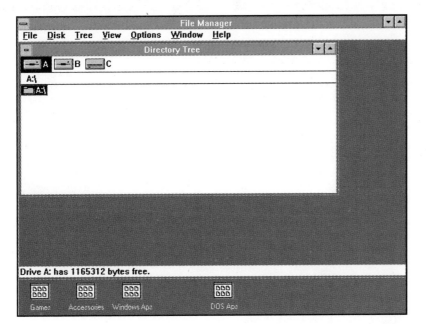

after

Return to drive C
To change the directory back to drive C, click on the disk drive C icon.

1. Open the **File Manager**.

2. Insert the floppy disk that you want to use into the drive.

3. Click on the icon for that drive.

To select a drive

Display files

before

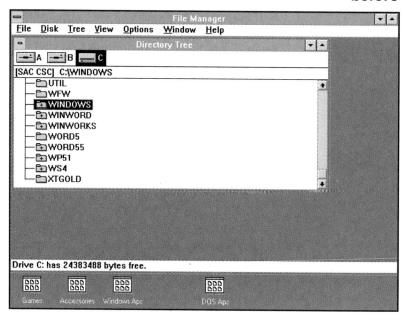

Oops!
To close the file display,
double-click on the
Control menu box for the
window. (Be sure that you
select the file list window.)

1. Open the **File Manager**.

To open the File Manager, double-click on the Main group icon. Then double-click on the File Manager icon. For more information on this step, see *TASK: Open the File Manager*.

The Directory Tree window appears. This window lists the directories in the root (or main) directory of drive C.

2. Point to the **WINDOWS** directory.

The WINDOWS directory contains the files that you want to display. (The Before screen shows this step.)

You may have to scroll through the list to find WINDOWS. The scroll arrows appear on the right side of the window.

3. Double-click on the **WINDOWS** directory name.

This step displays a list of directories and files that are contained in the WINDOWS directory. The directory name appears in the window's title bar (C:\WINDOWS*.*).

The window itself displays icons and names. Different entries have different icons. A directory entry, for example, is represented by a picture (or icon) of a folder. The directory name appears in brackets after the icon. A program file appears as a window with a title bar. Document files are squares with a folded corner.

Along the bottom of the file list window are right and left scroll arrows, which let you scroll through the display.

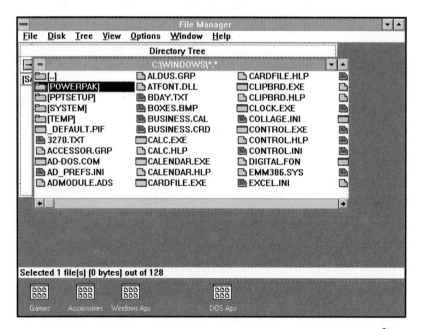

after

Manipulate the file list window
You can manipulate the file list window (move, resize, maximize, and so on) to display more or fewer files. See the tasks in the *Program Manager* section.

1. Open the **File Manager**.

2. Point to the name of the directory that contains the files you want to display.

3. Double-click the mouse button.

To display files

Display files in another directory
To open another window and display the files in another directory, double-click on that directory's name in the file list.

Display selected files

before

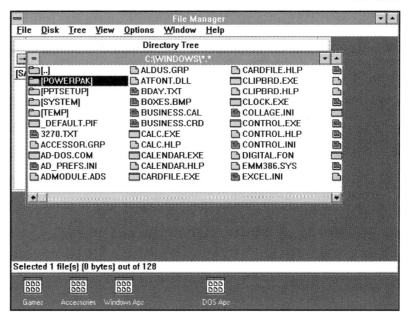

1. Open the **File Manager**.

To open the File Manager, double-click on the Main group icon. Then double-click on the File Manager icon. For more information on this step, see *TASK: Open the File Manager*.

The Directory Tree window appears. This window lists the directories in the root (or main) directory of drive C.

2. Double-click on the **WINDOWS** directory.

This step displays the files and directories in the WINDOWS directory. (The Before screen shows this step.)

You may have to scroll through the list to find WINDOWS. The scroll arrows appear on the right side of the window. To scroll, click on the scroll arrow that points in the direction that you want to scroll. To scroll down, for example, click on the down scroll arrow.

3. Click on **View** in the menu bar.

This step opens the View menu. You see the different options for viewing your files.

4. Click on **Include**.

This step selects the Include command. The Include dialog box appears, which enables you to specify the file types to include. The mouse pointer is positioned inside the Name text box. For more information on dialog boxes, see The Basics part of this book.

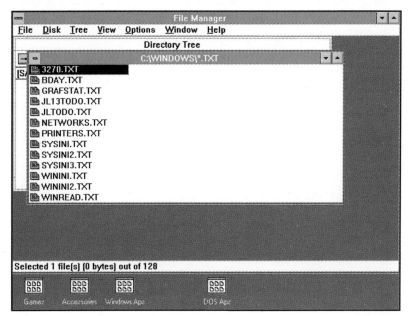

after

5. Type *.**txt**.

Typing **.txt* tells Microsoft Windows to display only files with the extension TXT. The files can have any name. The * is a wild card, which lets you specify groups of files, rather than naming each individual file.

6. Press **Enter**.

Pressing Enter confirms the selected name. The screen displays all the files in the WINDOWS directory that have the extension TXT.

REVIEW

To display selected files

1. Open the **File Manager**.

2. Point to the name of the directory that contains the files you want to display.

3. Double-click the mouse button.

4. Click on **View** in the menu bar.

5. Click on the **Include** command.

6. In the Name text box, type the name of the files that you want to include. You can type file names, extensions, or wild cards.

7. Press **Enter**.

Select a file

before

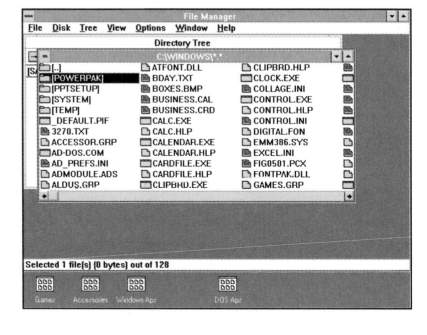

Oops!
If you click on the wrong file, deselect the file by clicking on another file.

1. **Open the File Manager.**

   To open the File Manager, double-click on the Main group icon. Then double-click on the File Manager icon. For more information on this step, see *TASK: Open the File Manager*.

   The Directory Tree window appears. This window lists the directories in the root (or main) directory of drive C.

2. **Double-click on the WINDOWS directory.**

   This step displays the files and directories in the WINDOWS directory. (The Before screen shows this step.)

   You may have to scroll through the list to find WINDOWS. The scroll arrows appear on the right side of the window. To scroll, click on the scroll arrow that points in the direction that you want to scroll. To scroll down, for example, click on the down scroll arrow.

3. **Point to the file BOXES.BMP and click the left mouse button.**

   This step selects the file BOXES.BMP. The file is highlighted on-screen. After you select the file, you can perform many operations on it, such as moving it, copying it, deleting it, and so on. See the other tasks in this section for more information.

   Your directory listing should include this file. If not, select a file that it does include.

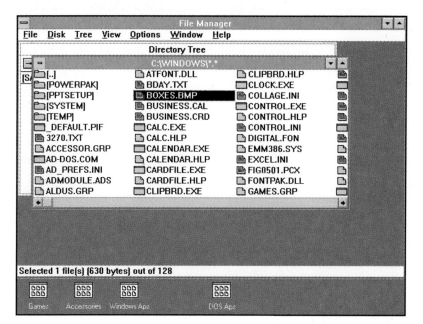

after

Select multiple files
You can also select multiple files. See *TASK: Select multiple files.*

1. Open the **File Manager**.

2. If necessary, expand the directory listing to display the directory that contains the file you want.

3. Double-click on the directory that contains the file.

4. Click on the file name.

To select a file

Select multiple files

before

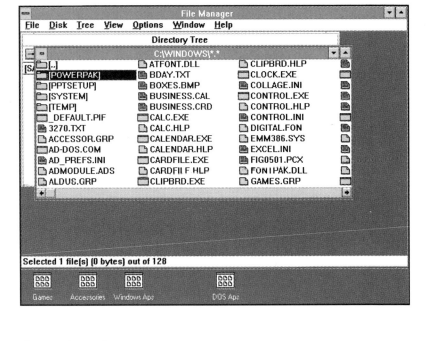

1. **Open the File Manager.**

   To open the File Manager, double-click on the Main group icon to open the Main program group window. Then double-click on the File Manager icon to start the File Manager. For more information on this step, see *TASK: Open the File Manager*.

   The Directory Tree window appears. This window lists the directories in the root (or main) directory of drive C.

2. **Double-click on the WINDOWS directory.**

   This step displays the files and directories in the WINDOWS directory. (The Before screen shows this step.)

   You may have to scroll through the list to find WINDOWS. The scroll arrows appear on the right side of the window. To scroll, click on the scroll arrow that points in the direction that you want to scroll. To scroll down, for example, click on the down scroll arrow.

3. **Point to the file BOXES.BMP and click the mouse button.**

   This step selects the BOXES.BMP file. The file highlights on-screen. Your directory listing should include this file. If not, select a file that it does include.

4. **Point to the file CHESS.BMP.**

   CHESS.BMP is the next file that you want to select. Your directory listing should include this file. If not, select a file that it does include.

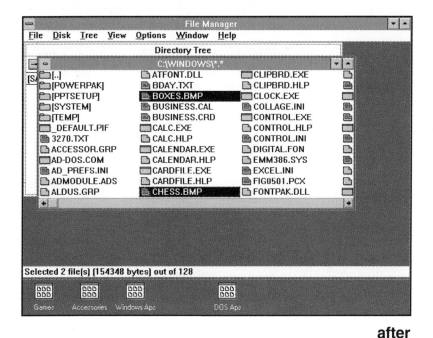

after

5. **Press and hold the Ctrl key and click the mouse button.**

   This step selects the second file without deselecting the first file. You can continue this process to select many files. After you select the files, you can perform operations on them. See the other tasks in this section for instructions.

REVIEW

1. Open the **File Manager**.

2. If necessary, expand the directory listing to display the directory that contains the file you want.

3. Double-click on the directory that contains the file.

4. Click on the first file name.

5. Point to the next file.

6. Press and hold the Ctrl key and click the mouse button.

7. Repeat steps 5 and 6 until you select all the files that you want.

To select multiple files

Select a set of files
Select a continuous set of files by clicking on the first file, pressing and holding the Shift key, and clicking on the last file.

Copy a file

before

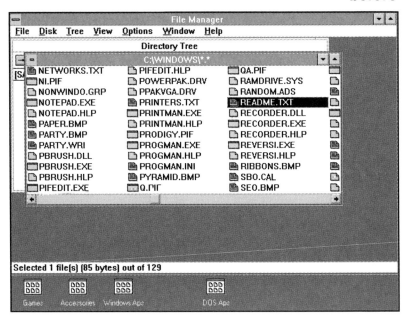

File Manager

File Disk Tree View Options Window Help

Directory Tree

C:\WINDOWS*.*

NETWORKS.TXT	PIFEDIT.HLP	QA.PIF
NI.PIF	POWERPAK.DRV	RAMDRIVE.SYS
NONWINDO.GRP	PPAKVGA.DRV	RANDOM.ADS
NOTEPAD.EXE	PRINTERS.TXT	README.TXT
NOTEPAD.HLP	PRINTMAN.EXE	RECORDER.DLL
PAPER.BMP	PRINTMAN.HLP	RECORDER.EXE
PARTY.BMP	PRODIGY.PIF	RECORDER.HLP
PARTY.WRI	PROGMAN.EXE	REVERSI.EXE
PBRUSH.DLL	PROGMAN.HLP	REVERSI.HLP
PBRUSH.EXE	PROGMAN.INI	RIBBONS.BMP
PBRUSH.HLP	PYRAMID.BMP	SBO.CAL
PIFEDIT.EXE	Q.PIF	SEO.BMP

Selected 1 file[s] [85 bytes] out of 129

Games   Accessories Windows Apps   DOS Apps

Oops!

If you change your mind, click on Cancel instead of Copy in step 5 or step 7 of the Task section.

1. **Open the File Manager.**

   To open the File Manager, double-click on the Main group icon. Then double-click on the File Manager icon. The Directory Tree window appears. This window lists the directories in the root (or main) directory of drive C.

2. **Double-click on the WINDOWS directory.**

   This step displays the files and directories in the WINDOWS directory.

   You may have to scroll through the list to find WINDOWS. The scroll arrows appear on the right side of the window. To scroll, click on the scroll arrow that points in the direction that you want to scroll.

3. **Point to the file README.TXT and click the mouse button.**

   This step selects the file README.TXT. (The Before screen shows this step.) You may have to scroll through the list to find this file.

4. **Click on File in the menu bar.**

   This step opens the File menu. You see a list of File commands.

5. **Click on Copy.**

   This step selects the Copy command. The Copy dialog box appears, which includes the current directory name and two text boxes. The first text box is named From: and displays the selected file. The second text box is named To:. The mouse pointer is positioned inside the To: box. You use this box to enter the name for the copy that you are creating.

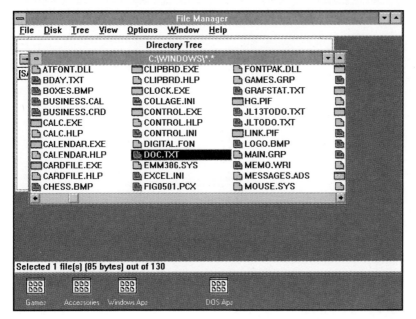

after

6. Type **DOC.TXT**.

   DOC.TXT is the name of the file that you want to create. You will have two copies of the same file: README.TXT and DOC.TXT.

7. Click on **Copy**.

   This step tells Microsoft Windows to make a copy of the file. In the directory listing, you see the new file DOC.TXT.

REVIEW

1. Open the **File Manager**.

2. If necessary, expand the directory listing to display the directory that contains the file you want to copy.

3. Double-click on the directory that contains the file.

4. Click on the name of the file that you want to copy.

5. Click on **File** in the menu bar.

6. Click on the **Copy** command.

7. Type the new file's name in the To: text box and press **Enter**.

Copy to different drive or directory
You can copy the file to a different drive or directory by typing the path name (drive, directory, and file name) in the To: text box.

To copy a file

Use a shortcut
You also can press F8 to select the File Copy command.

Delete a file

before

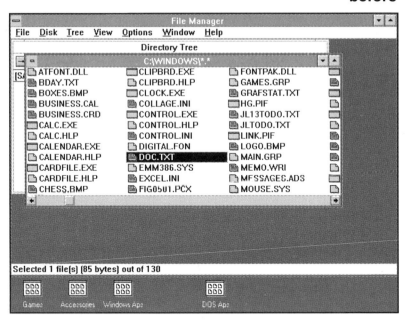

Oops!
If you change your mind about deleting a file, click on Cancel in step 7 of the Task section.

1. **Open the File Manager.**

   To open the File Manager, double-click on the Main group icon. Then double-click on the File Manager icon. The Directory Tree window appears. This window lists the directories in the root (or main) directory of drive C.

2. **Double-click on the WINDOWS directory.**

   This step displays the files and directories in the WINDOWS directory.

   You may have to scroll through the list to find WINDOWS. The scroll arrows appear on the right side of the window. To scroll, click on the scroll arrow that points in the direction that you want to scroll.

3. **Point to the file DOC.TXT and click the mouse button.**

   This step selects the DOC.TXT file. (The Before screen shows this step.) If you don't have this file (created in *TASK: Copy a file*), select a file that you do not need.

4. **Click on File in the menu bar.**

   This step opens the File menu. You see a list of File commands.

5. **Click on Delete.**

   This step selects the Delete command. The Delete dialog box appears. You see the current directory name and the Delete text box. The selected file appears in the text box.

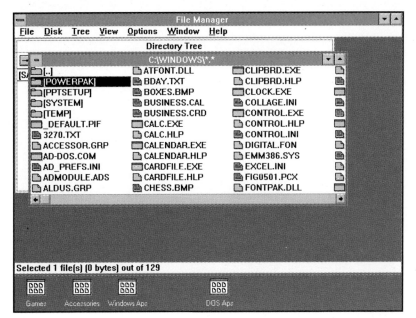

after

6. **Click on Delete.**

   Clicking on the Delete button tells Windows that you want to delete the selected file. You see an alert box that says `Delete file C:\WINDOWS\DOC.TXT.`

7. **Click on Yes.**

   Clicking on Yes confirms that you want to delete the file DOC.TXT. Microsoft Windows deletes the file.

REVIEW

1. Open the **File Manager**.

2. If necessary, expand the directory listing to display the directory that contains the file you want.

3. Double-click on the directory that contains the file.

4. Click on the file name that you want to delete.

5. Click on **File** in the menu bar.

6. Click on the **Delete** command.

7. Click on the **Delete** button.

8. Click on **Yes**.

To delete a file

Use a shortcut
You can also press Del to select the File Delete command.

Rename a file

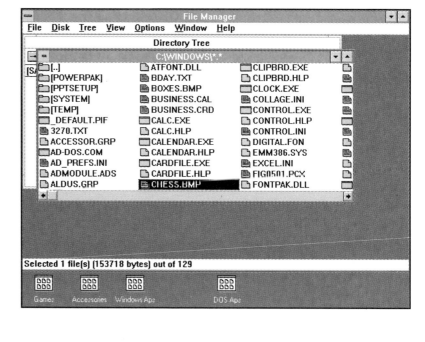

Oops!
To rename the file back to its original name, follow this same procedure.

1. **Open the File Manager.**

   To open the File Manager, double-click on the Main group icon. Then double-click on the File Manager icon. The Directory Tree window appears. This window lists the directories in the root (or main) directory of drive C.

2. **Double-click on the WINDOWS directory.**

   Double-clicking displays the files and directories in the WINDOWS directory. You may have to scroll through the list to find WINDOWS. The scroll arrows appear on the right side of the window. To scroll, click on the scroll arrow that points in the direction that you want to scroll.

3. **Point to the file CHESS.BMP and click the mouse button.**

   This step selects the file CHESS.BMP. The file is highlighted on-screen. (The Before screen shows this step.) Your directory listing should include this file. If not, select a file that it does include.

4. **Click on File in the menu bar.**

   This step opens the File menu. You see a list of File commands.

5. **Click on Rename.**

   This step selects the Rename command. Inside the Rename dialog box, you see the current directory name and two text boxes. The first text box is named From: and displays the selected file. The second text box is named To:. The mouse pointer is positioned inside the To: box, and you type the new file name in this box.

Easy **Windows**

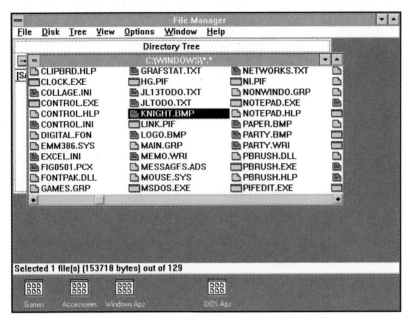

after

6. Type **KNIGHT.BMP**.

    KNIGHT.BMP is the new name that you want to assign the file.

7. Press **Enter**.

    Pressing Enter confirms the new name. The file appears in the current directory listing under its new name. You may have to scroll through the file list to see the name.

R E V I E W

To rename a file

1. Open the **File Manager**.

2. If necessary, expand the directory listing to display the directory that contains the file you want.

3. Double-click on the directory that contains the file.

4. Click on the name of the file that you want to rename.

5. Click on **File** in the menu bar.

6. Click on the **Rename** command.

7. Type the new name in the To: text box.

8. Press **Enter**.

Cancel the renaming
If you change your mind about renaming the file, click Cancel in the Rename dialog box before you press Enter.

Move a file

before

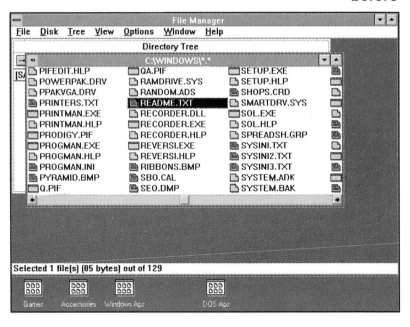

Oops!
Follow this same procedure to move the file back to its original location. To select the file, display the files in the TEMP directory and type *C:\WINDOWS* in the To: text box.

1. **Open the File Manager.**

   To open the File Manager, double-click on the Main group icon. Then double-click on the File Manager icon. For more information on this step, see *TASK: Open the File Manager.*

   The Directory Tree window appears. This window lists the directories in the root (or main) directory of drive C.

2. **Double-click on the WINDOWS directory.**

   This step displays the files and directories in the WINDOWS directory.

   You may have to scroll through the list to find WINDOWS. The scroll arrows appear on the right side of the window.

3. **Point to the file README.TXT and click the mouse button.**

   This step selects the file, and the file is highlighted on-screen. (The Before screen shows this step.) Your directory listing should include this file. If not, select a file that it does include.

4. **Click on File in the menu bar.**

   This step opens the File menu. You see a list of File commands.

5. **Click on Move.**

   This step displays the Move dialog box. Inside this dialog box, you see the current directory name and two text boxes. The first text box is named From: and displays the selected file. The second text box is named To:. The mouse pointer is positioned inside the To: box, and you type the location where you want to move the file in this box.

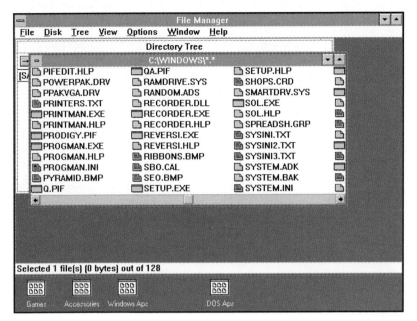

after

Be careful!
Do not move a file that
must be in a specific
directory. For example,
don't move any program
files (files with the
extension COM, EXE,
PIF, or BAT).

6. Type **C:\WINDOWS\TEMP**.

   C:\WINDOWS\TEMP is the location where you want to move the file.
   With this command, you are moving the file to the TEMP directory,
   which is a subdirectory of the WINDOWS directory.

   If you don't have a TEMP directory, type a directory that you do have.

7. Press **Enter**.

   Pressing Enter moves the file entry to the new directory. The entry
   no longer appears in the current directory listing.

REVIEW

To move a file

1. Open the **File Manager**.

2. If necessary, expand the directory listing to display the
   directory that contains the file you want.

3. Double-click on the directory that contains the file.

4. Click on the name of the file that you want to move.

5. Click on **File** in the menu bar.

6. Click on the **Move** command.

7. In the To: text box, type the location where you want to
   move the file and press **Enter**.

Use a shortcut
You can also press the F7
key to select the File
Move command.

Search for a file

before

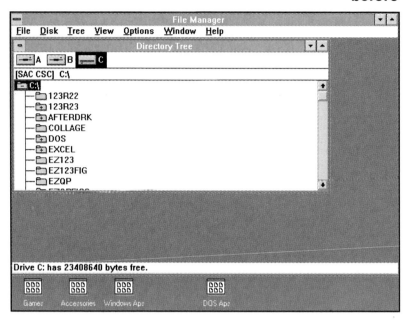

Oops!
If the search does not find the requested file, you may have typed the name incorrectly.

1. **Open the File Manager.**

   To open the File Manager, double-click on the Main group icon. Then double-click on the File Manager icon. For more information on this step, see *TASK: Open the File Manager*.

   The Directory Tree window appears. This window lists the directories in the root (or main) directory of drive C.

2. **Click on File in the menu bar.**

   This step opens the File menu. You see a list of File commands.

3. **Click on Search.**

   This step selects the Search command. The Search dialog box appears. The current directory is listed at the top of the dialog box. The Search For: text box contains *.*. (The mouse pointer is positioned inside this box.) Also notice the Search Entire Disk box. When this box contains an X, Windows searches your entire disk for the selected file.

4. **Type CLOCK.EXE.**

   CLOCK.EXE is the name of the file that you want to find. If you do not know the entire name of the file, you can use wild cards in the search. For example, you could specify this file by typing *CLOCK**. Microsoft Windows would find every file named CLOCK, regardless of the file extension.

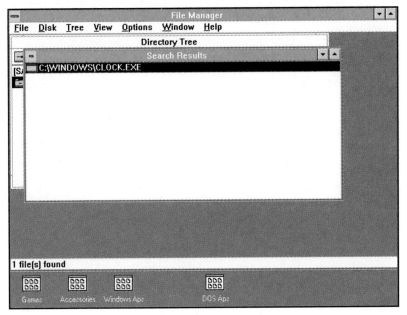

after

What is a wild card?
A wild card is a character that lets you specify a group of files. For more information, see your Windows manual or *Using Microsoft Windows 3,* 2nd Edition.

5. Press **Enter**.

Pressing the Enter key confirms the name and starts the search. Windows looks through all directories for files that match this name. When it finds a file, it displays the Search Results window. You see C:\WINDOWS\CLOCK.EXE, which tells you the location or path to the file. CLOCK.EXE is stored in the WINDOWS directory on drive C.

For other searches, Windows may find several entries. All matching entries are listed.

6. Double-click on the **Control menu box** for this window.

This step closes the Search Results window.

REVIEW

1. Open the **File Manager**.

2. Click on **File** in the menu bar.

3. Click on the **Search** command.

4. Type the file name that you want to find. You can use wild cards.

5. Press **Enter**.

6. Double-click on the **Control menu box** for the Search Results window to close the window.

To search for a file

File Manager

Create a directory

before

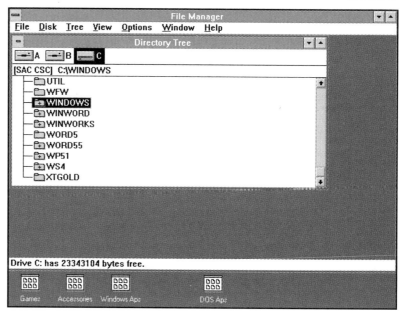

Oops!

Remember that you are creating a directory within a directory. Be sure to point to the first directory before creating the new directory.

1. **Open the File Manager.**

   To open the File Manager, double-click on the Main group icon. Then double-click on the File Manager icon. For more information on this step, see *TASK: Open the File Manager.*

   The Directory Tree window appears. This window lists the directories in the root (or main) directory of drive C.

2. **Click on the WINDOWS directory.**

   This step selects WINDOWS as the current directory. (The Before screen shows this step.)

   You may have to scroll through the list to find WINDOWS. The scroll arrows appear on the right side of the window. To scroll, click on the scroll arrow that points in the direction that you want to scroll. To scroll down, for example, click on the down scroll arrow.

3. **Click on File in the menu bar.**

   This step opens the File menu. You see a list of File commands.

4. **Click on Create Directory.**

   This step displays the Create Directory dialog box. This dialog box lists the current directory name and contains the Name: text box. The mouse pointer is positioned inside this text box.

5. **Type DATA.**

   DATA is the name of the directory that you want to create. This directory will be a subdirectory of the WINDOWS directory.

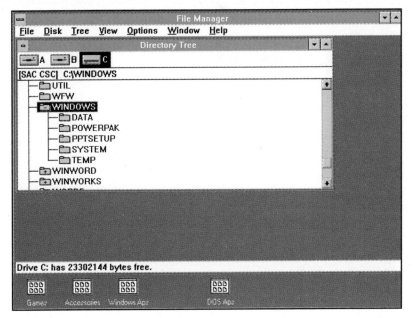

after

Make a directory from the root directory
If you want to make the directory a branch of the root directory, select C:\ in the Directory Tree window.

6. Press **Enter**.

   Pressing Enter confirms the name and creates the directory. You return to the WINDOWS directory.

7. Click on the **WINDOWS** directory icon.

   This step expands the directories to show subdirectories. You see the new subdirectory DATA.

REVIEW

1. Open the **File Manager**.

2. Click on the directory in which you want to place the new directory. Click on **C:** to select the root directory.

3. Click on **File** in the menu bar.

4. Click on the **Create Directory** command.

5. Type the directory name.

6. Press **Enter**.

To create a directory

Remove a directory
To remove the new directory, see *TASK: Remove directory.*

Remove a directory

before

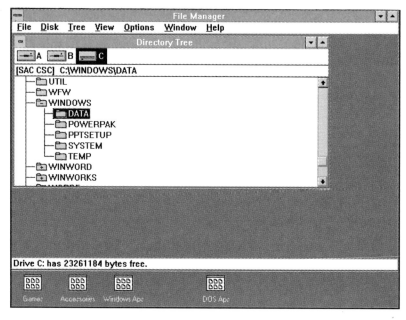

Oops!
If you are unsure whether
you want to remove the
directory, click on Cancel
in step 6 or step 7 of the
Task section.

1. Open the **File Manager**.

To open the File Manager, double-click on the Main group icon. Then double-click on the File Manager icon. For more information on this step, see *TASK: Open the File Manager*.

The Directory Tree window appears. This window lists the directories in the root (or main) directory of drive C.

2. Click on the **WINDOWS** directory icon.

This step expands the directory so that you can see the DATA directory. (The Before screen shows this step.) If the directory listing is already expanded, skip this step.

3. Click on the **DATA** directory name.

DATA is the directory that you want to delete. If you don't have this directory, select one that you do have. Be sure to select a directory that you do not need.

The DATA directory should be empty. If not, you may want to create an empty directory for this exercise. See *TASK: Create a directory*.

You cannot remove a directory unless all the files in that directory are deleted. If the directory contains files or other directories and you try to delete it, Windows prompts you to confirm the deletion of each file and directory. You must answer Yes and delete all files and directories before the directory is removed.

4. Click on **File** in the menu bar.

This step opens the File menu. You see a list of File commands.

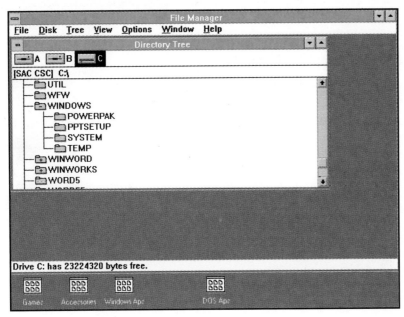

after

5. Click on **Delete**.

   This step displays the Delete dialog box. The directory name is listed in this box.

6. Click on **Delete**.

   Clicking on the Delete button tells Windows that you want to delete the selected directory. You see an alert box that asks `Remove subtree C:\WINDOWS\DATA?`

7. Click on **Yes**.

   Clicking on Yes confirms the removal of the directory. Scroll through the directory tree window until you see that the subdirectories for WINDOWS. DATA is no longer listed.

REVIEW

1. Open the **File Manager**.

2. Select the directory that you want to delete.

3. Click on **File** in the menu bar.

4. Click on the **Delete** command.

5. Click on the **Delete** button.

6. Click on the **Yes** button.

To remove a directory

Close the File Manager

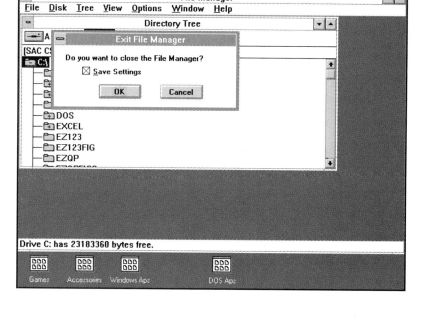

Oops!
If you change your mind about closing the File Manager, click on Cancel in step 2.

1. **Double-click on the Control menu box for the File Manager.**

   This step displays the Exit File Manager dialog box. You see the prompt Do you want to close the File Manager?

2. **Click on OK.**

   Clicking on OK closes the File Manager and all directory windows. The Main window is still open on-screen, and the Program Manager is still running.

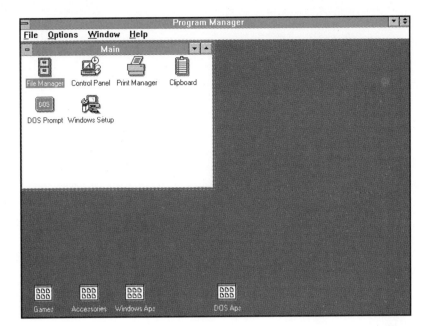

after

Remember...
Although the Directory Tree window has a Control menu box, you cannot close this window unless you close the File Manager.

1. Double-click on the **Control menu box**.

2. Click on **OK**.

To close the File Manager

Save settings
When an X appears in the Save Settings box of the Exit File Manager dialog box, certain settings from this work session are retained. Click on the box to turn this on and off.

Accessory Programs

This section covers the following tasks:

Run a program

Switch to a different program

Exit a program

Use the Calculator

Display the time

Add an appointment

Save a calendar file

Open a calendar file

Edit an appointment

Set an alarm

Delete an appointment

Create a note

Open a note

Edit a note

Print a note

Create a cardfile

Save a cardfile

Open a cardfile

Add cards

Edit a card

Find a card

Print all cards

Delete a card

Start Windows Write

Create a Write document

Save a Write document

Open a Write document

Edit a Write document

Cut and paste text

Center text

Make text bold

Indent text

Find text

Print a Write document

Start Windows Paintbrush

Create a Paintbrush drawing

Save a Paintbrush drawing

Open a Paintbrush drawing

Edit a drawing

Run a program

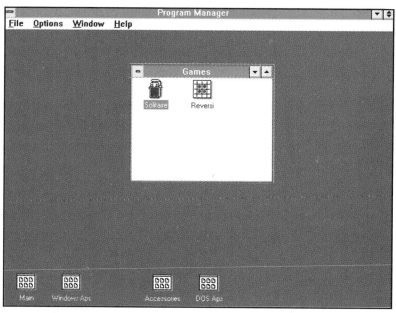

before

Oops!
If the program doesn't start, you may not have clicked twice. Point to the icon again and press the mouse button twice in rapid succession.

1. **Close all group windows so that only the program group icons are displayed.**

   You do not have to follow this step, but doing so enables you to find the group icon that you need easily. For help with this step, see *TASK: Close a window*.

2. **Double-click on the Games group icon.**

   This step opens the Games program window. (The Before screen shows this step.) The Microsoft Windows package includes two games: Solitaire and Reversi. Both games appear in the Games window.

3. **Double-click on the Solitaire icon.**

   This step starts the Solitaire program. You see the cards on-screen.

   For information on playing Solitaire, see your Microsoft Windows manual or *Using Microsoft Windows 3,* 2nd Edition.

Easy **Windows**

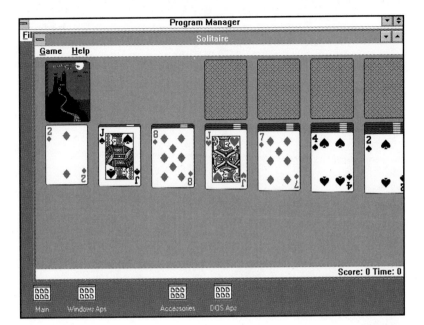

after

Exit the program
To exit a Microsoft Windows program, double-click on the Control menu box.

1. Open the group window that contains the program.

2. Double-click on the program icon.

To run a program

Save changes
If you make changes while in a program, you are prompted to save the changes when you exit. Follow the save procedures for that program.

Switch to a different program

before

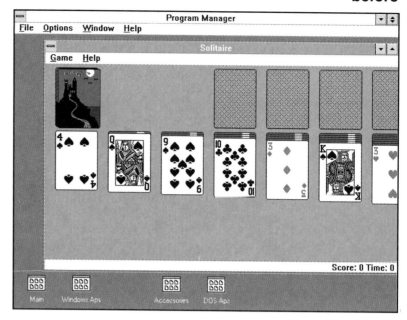

Oops!
To switch back to the original program, follow this same procedure.

1. **Start the Solitaire program.**

   To start the program, double-click on the Games icon. Then double-click on the Solitaire icon to start the Solitaire program. For help with the step, see *TASK: Run a program*.

   Remember that the Program Manager is also a program. You now have two programs running.

2. **Click on the Control menu box for the Solitaire window.**

   This step opens the Control menu.

3. **Click on Switch To.**

   This step selects the Switch To command. You see the Task List dialog box. Within that box, you see a list of programs that are currently running.

4. **Click on Program Manager.**

   This step selects the Program Manager.

5. **Click on Switch To.**

   This step selects the Switch To button. The Solitaire window disappears, and you return to the Program Manager. The Solitaire window is still open and the program is still running, even though it appears as an icon on-screen.

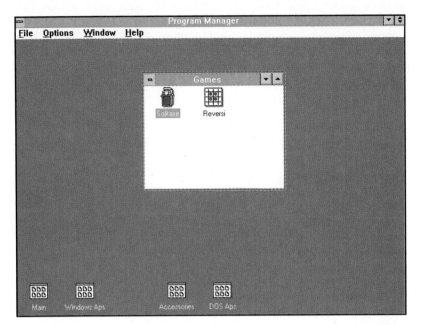

after

Use other programs
You can run many different Microsoft Windows programs many different ways. See your Microsoft Windows manual or *Using Microsoft Windows 3*, 2nd Edition.

REVIEW

1. Click on the Control menu box for the current program.

2. Click on the Switch To command.

3. Select the program that you want from the Task List.

4. Click on the Switch To button.

To switch to a different program

Exit a program

before

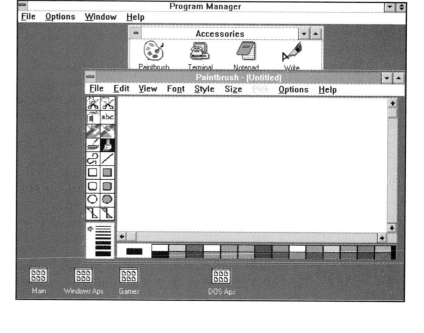

Oops!
Be sure that you save your work before you close a program. If you don't, you are reminded to save.

1. Close all group windows so that only the group icons are displayed.

   You do not have to follow this step, but doing so enables you to find the group icon that you need. For help with this step, see *TASK: Close a window.*

2. Point to the **Accessories** icon and double-click the mouse button.

   This step opens the Accessories window. You see icons for the accessory programs.

   To exit a program, you have to first start it. For this exercise, you start the Paintbrush program, which is in the Accessories window.

3. Point to the **Paintbrush** program icon and double-click the mouse.

   This step selects and starts the program. You see the Paintbrush draw screen. (Although this book does not cover all the Paintbrush options, it does include some basic tasks. For complete information on using this program, see your Microsoft Windows manual or *Using Microsoft Windows 3*, 2nd Edition.)

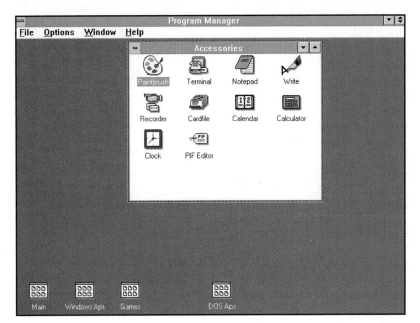

after

4. Double-click on the **Control menu box**.

   This step closes the program. The Accessories window is still open on-screen.

Double-click on the **Control menu box**.

To exit a program

Exiting vs. minimizing
Exiting is different from minimizing. When you minimize a program, you restore it to an icon, but the program is still running in memory. See *TASK: Minimize a window.*

Use the File Exit command
Most programs have a File Exit or similar command. You can also use this command to exit a program.

Use the Calculator

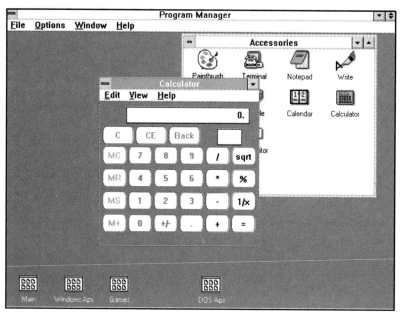

1. **Start the Calculator.**

   The Calculator is stored in the Accessories program group. Open this group window by double-clicking on the Accessories group icon. Then double-click on the icon for the Calculator. For more information on starting a program, see *TASK: Run a program*.

   You see an on-screen version of a calculator. The Calculator has number keys, operator keys (plus, minus, and so on), and other keys. You can enter numbers by typing them from the keyboard or by pointing to them and clicking the mouse button. Use the Calculator as you would a regular calculator.

2. **Type 2400.**

   2400 is the first value that you want to enter. You see this value on the entry line of the Calculator.

3. **Type /.**

   The forward slash (/) is the division key. This tells the calculator that you want to divide 2400 by a number. The entry line still displays 2400.

4. **Type 12.**

   12 is the number by which you want to divide 2400. The equation you have entered is 2400/12, but you see just the number 12 on the entry line.

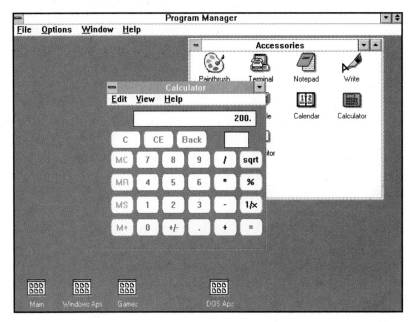

after

Close the Calculator
To close the Calculator, double-click on the Control menu box for that window. Notice that you cannot resize the Calculator window.

5. Press **Enter**.

   Pressing the Enter key tells Microsoft Windows to calculate the formula. You see the result in the entry line (200).

6. Press **Esc**.

   Pressing the Esc key clears the entry line so that you can enter another equation.

To use the Calculator

1. Start the Calculator.

2. Type the value that you want to enter. Or click on the value in the number pad on-screen.

3. Type or click on the mathematical operator that you want (+, –, *, /, and so on).

4. Type the next value.

5. Continue typing values and operators until you complete the equation.

6. Press **Enter**.

Display the time

before

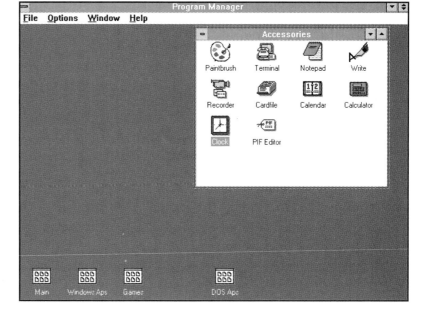

Oops!
To close the clock window, double-click on the Control menu box for that window.

1. **Double-click on the Accessories group icon.**

   This step opens the Accessories group window. You see program icons for all the accessory programs. The clock is stored in this group window.

2. **Double-click on the Clock icon.**

   This step starts the Clock program. On-screen you see a clock that displays the current time.

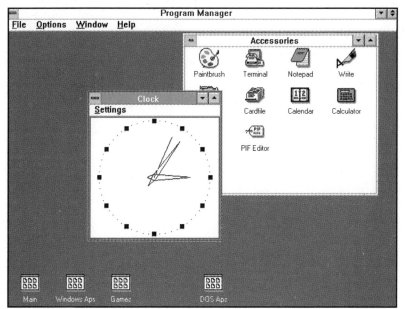

after

Change clock format
You can change the clock
format from analog (a
clock face) to digital
(numeric readout).
See *Using Microsoft
Windows 3*, 2nd Edition,
for more information.

REVIEW

1. Double-click on the **Accessories** group icon.

2. Double-click on the **Clock** icon.

To display the time

Minimize the clock
If you minimize the clock,
the current time is shown
on the icon. See *TASK:
Minimize a window*.

Add an appoint-ment

before

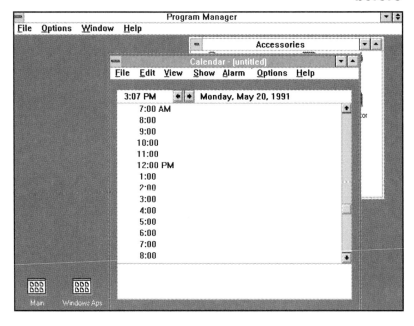

Oops!
To delete an appointment, see *TASK: Delete an appointment.*

1. **Start the Calendar accessory.**

   You use the Calendar accessory to enter appointments. To start Calendar, double-click on the Accessories group icon. Then double-click on the Calendar icon. For information on this step, see *TASK: Run a program.*

   You see an appointment listing for the current date. The current date and time are displayed at the top of the window under the menu bar. Between the date and time, you also see two scroll arrows. You use these arrows to scroll from date to date.

   Along the right of the window are two other scroll arrows. You use these arrows to scroll to a different time.

   The default appointment list includes appointment slots for each hour. You can change the increment of the slots; you could display appointments every 15 minutes, for example. For information, see *Using Microsoft Windows 3*, 2nd Edition.

2. **Click the right-arrow key that is next to the date.**

   This step displays the next day's date. (The current date will be different from the one that you see in the Before and After screens.)

3. **Click on 12:00 PM.**

   This step moves the flashing insertion point to the right of 12:00 PM. You want to enter an appointment for this time.

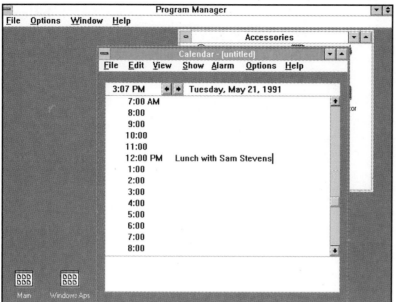

after

Add other appointments
If you have saved and closed the file and want to add appointments, open the file first. See *TASK: Open a calendar file.*

4. Type **Lunch with Sam Stevens**.

   This text describes the appointment you are entering. The text can be up to 80 characters long.

   You can continue to add other appointments. After you finish, you must save the calendar file. See *TASK: Save a calendar file.*

1. Start the **Calendar** accessory.

2. Scroll to the date on which you want to enter an appointment by clicking on the scroll arrows at the top of the calendar.

3. Click on the time for the appointment.

4. Type the text for the appointment.

5. Save the calendar file.

To add an appoint-ment

Set an alarm
You can also set an alarm to remind you of appointments. See *TASK: Set an alarm.*

Save a calendar file

before

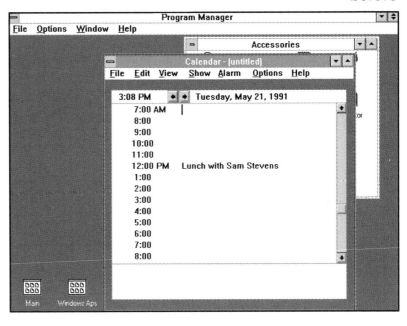

Oops!
To close the Calendar, save the calendar file and then double-click on the Control menu box.

1. **Start the Calendar accessory.**

   To start Calendar, double-click on the Accessories group icon. Then double-click on the Calendar icon. For information on this step, see *TASK: Run a program*.

2. **Enter appointments.**

   See *TASK: Add an appointment* for help with this step.

   If you have entered appointments already, you can skip steps 1 and 2.

3. **Click on File in the menu bar.**

   This step opens the File menu. All appointments are saved in a calendar file. You can keep several calendar files. You might have one to keep track of projects and one to keep track of personal appointments, for example.

4. **Click on Save.**

   This step selects the Save command and displays the File Save As dialog box. Inside this box you see a Filename text box. (The mouse pointer is positioned inside this text box.) The current directory and a list of directories are listed in the dialog box.

5. **Type BUSINESS.**

   BUSINESS is the name you want to assign to the calendar file. The name can be up to eight characters long and cannot contain spaces. As a general rule, use only alphanumeric characters.

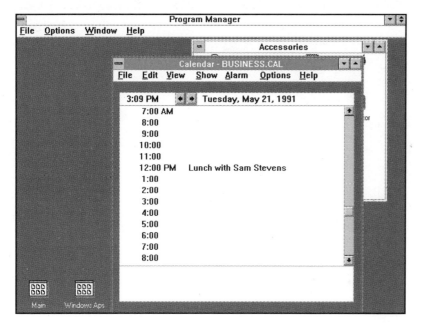

after

Save the calendar again
After you have saved the file for the first time, simply click on File and then Save to save the file again. The file is saved with the same name.

6. Press **Enter**.

Pressing Enter saves the file. The file is saved with the extension CAL. The calendar file remains on-screen, and the name that you just typed appears in the title bar.

R E V I E W

1. Start the **Calendar** accessory.

2. Enter the appointment(s).

3. Click on **File** in the menu bar.

4. Click on the **Save** command.

5. Type a file name.

6. Press **Enter**.

To save a calendar file

Open a calendar file

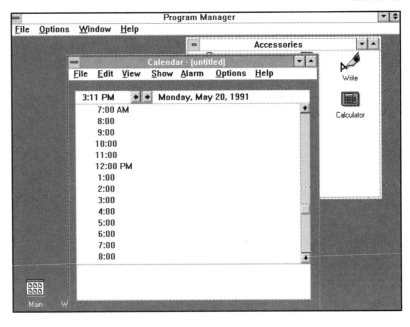

Oops!
To close the Calendar,
save the calendar file and
then double-click on the
Control menu box for the
Calendar window.

1. **Start the Calendar accessory.**

   To start Calendar, double-click on the Accessories group icon. Then double-click on the Calendar icon. For information on this step, see *TASK: Run a program.*

   You see a blank appointment listing for the current date. Every time that you start the Calendar accessory, a new, blank calendar file is opened. This file does not contain any entries. To review or edit appointments, open the calendar file first.

2. **Click on File in the menu bar.**

   This step opens the File menu. You see a list of File commands.

3. **Click on Open.**

   This step selects the Open command. You see the File Open dialog box. This dialog box includes a Filename text box. (The mouse pointer is positioned inside this text box.) The dialog box also lists the current entry. You also see two list boxes: a files list and a directory list.

4. **Type BUSINESS.**

   BUSINESS is the name of the file that you want to open. You can also select the file by clicking on the file name in the Files list box.

5. **Press Enter.**

   Pressing Enter confirms the file name and opens the calendar file. The appointment listings for the current date appear on-screen. If no appointments appear, you didn't schedule any for that day.

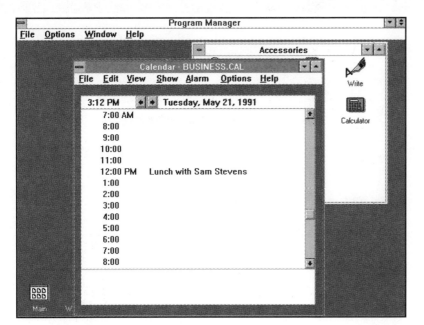

after

Display other dates
To scroll to other dates, click on the scroll arrows below the menu bar.

REVIEW

1. Start the **Calendar** accessory.

2. Click on **File** in the menu bar.

3. Click on the **Open** command.

4. Type the name of the file that you want to open.

5. Press **Enter**.

To open a calendar file

Try a shortcut
You can also open a file by pointing to the file name with the mouse pointer and then double-clicking the mouse button.

Edit an appoint- ment

before

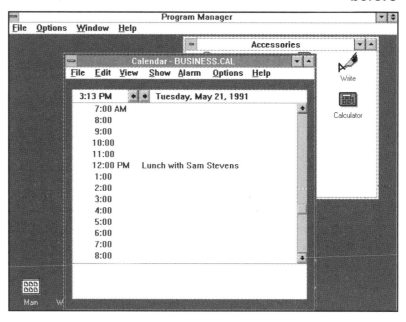

Oops!
To close the Calendar, save the calendar file and then double-click on the Control menu box.

1. **Start the Calendar accessory.**

   To start Calendar, open the Accessories program group by double-clicking on the group icon. Then start the program by double-clicking on the Calendar icon. For information on this step, see *TASK: Run a program*.

2. **Open the BUSINESS file.**

   See *TASK: Open a calendar file* for help with this step. If you do not have a file named BUSINESS, open a file that you do have.

3. **Use the scroll arrows to find the date with the appointment for lunch with Sam Stevens.**

   If you don't have this appointment, scroll to any existing appointment.

4. **Click after the last *s* in *Stevens*.**

   The *s* marks the end of the current appointment entry.

5. **Press the space bar.**

   Pressing the space bar inserts a space between the current text and the text you are about to type.

6. **Type and Max Moore.**

   The previous text scrolls off-screen. This text is still part of the appointment entry; although you don't see the entire entry. The appointment entry is now complete.

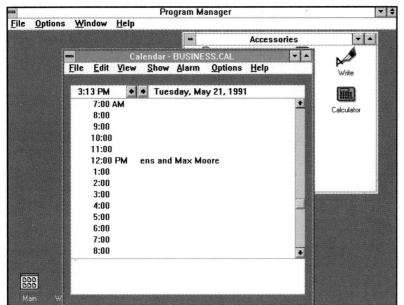

after

Remember...
Every time you start
the Calendar, a blank
calendar file is opened.
To find your appoint-
ments, you must open the
appropriate calendar file.

7. Click on **File** and then **Save**.

   This step opens the File menu and selects the Save command. The
   edited version of the file is saved to disk, and the file remains on-
   screen. (See *TASK: Save a calendar file* for more information on
   this step.)

1. Start the **Calendar** accessory.

2. Open the calendar file that contains the appointment
   you want to edit.

3. Use the scroll arrows near the top of the window to
   move to the date of the appointment.

4. Click next to the appointment that you want to edit.

5. Make any changes.

6. Click on **File** and then **Save** to save the calendar file.

**To edit an
appoint-
ment**

Set an alarm

before

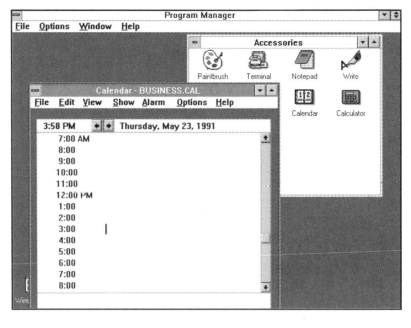

Oops!
To turn off the alarm, click on the appointment time and select Alarm Set.

1. **Start the Calendar accessory.**

    To start Calendar, double-click on the Accessories program group icon. Then double-click on the Calendar icon. For information on this step, see *TASK: Run a program*.

2. **Open the BUSINESS calendar file.**

    See *TASK: Open a calendar file* for help with this step. If you do not have a calendar file called BUSINESS, open a calendar file that you do have. You see the appointment listing for the current date.

3. **Click the scroll arrows until you move to a Thursday date.**

    The date for the Thursday will differ, depending on the current date (the date on which you start).

4. **Click on 3:00 PM.**

    You can set an alarm on an appointment that you have entered already or on a new appointment. You will enter a new appointment.

5. **Type Board Meeting.**

    Board Meeting describes the appointment.

6. **Click on Alarm in the menu bar.**

    This step opens the Alarm menu.

7. **Click on Set.**

    This step selects the Set command. Next to the appointment time, you see a bell.

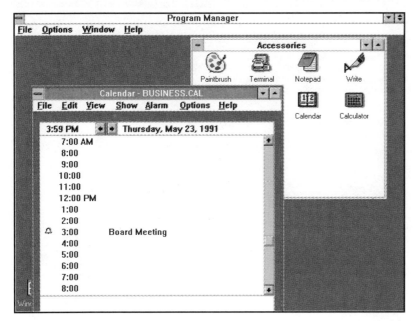

after

Add an alarm
You can add an alarm to an existing appointment by displaying that appointment, clicking on it, and selecting Alarm Set. See *TASK: Edit an appointment.*

8. Click on **File** and then **Save**.

This step opens the File menu, selects the Save command, and saves the calendar file. See *TASK: Save a calendar file* for more information on this step.

For the alarm to sound, you must have the Calendar accessory running with either the window open or the program minimized to an icon. If you do not start this accessory, the alarm will not alert you when it should.

If Calendar is running, you hear a beep at the appointment time. If the window is open, a dialog box appears that reminds you of the appointment. Click OK to close the dialog box.

REVIEW

1. Start the **Calendar** accessory.

2. Enter a new appointment or display an existing appointment.

3. Click on the appointment.

4. Click on **Alarm**.

5. Click on **Set**.

6. Click on **File** and then **Save** to save the calendar file.

To set an alarm

Try a shortcut
You can also set an alarm by moving the mouse pointer to the appointment for which you want to set an alarm and pressing the F5 key.

Delete an appointment

before

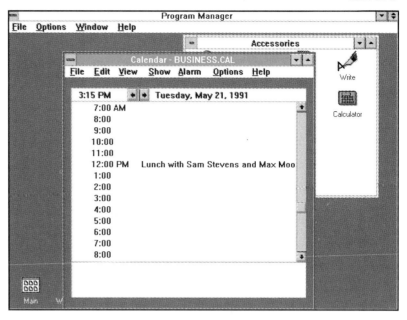

1. Start the **Calendar** accessory.

   To start Calendar, double-click on the Accessories program group icon. Then double-click on the Calendar icon. For information on this step, see *TASK: Run a program*.

2. Open the **BUSINESS** calendar file.

   If you don't have a calendar file named BUSINESS, open one that you do have. See *TASK: Open a calendar file* for help with this step.

3. Use the scroll arrows near the top of the window to find the date with the appointment for lunch with Sam Stevens and Max Moore.

   If you do not have this appointment, find one that you do have.

4. Point to the *L* in *Lunch*.

   This step positions the mouse pointer at the beginning of the text that you want to delete. To delete an appointment, you delete the entire text.

5. Press and hold the mouse button, and then drag the mouse across all the text.

   This step selects the text for the appointment.

   For more information about mouse procedures, see the section *Using a Mouse* in The Basics part of this book.

6. Press the Del key.

   Pressing the Del key deletes the selected text.

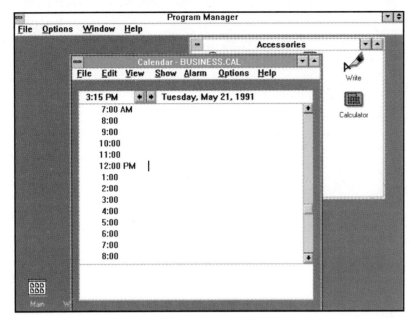

after

7. Click on **File** and then **Save**.

   This step opens the File menu, selects the Save command, and saves the calendar file. See *TASK: Save a calendar file* for more information.

1. Start the **Calendar** accessory.

2. Open the calendar file that contains the appointment you want to delete.

3. Use the scroll arrows near the top of the window to move to the date of the appointment.

4. Select the appointment text that you want to delete.

5. Delete the appointment text.

6. Click on **File** and then **Save** to save the calendar file.

Remove several appointments
You can remove all appointments within a certain date range. See *Using Microsoft Windows 3*, 2nd Edition, for more information.

To delete an appointment

Close Calendar
To close the calendar, save the calendar file and then double-click on the Control menu box.

Create a note

before

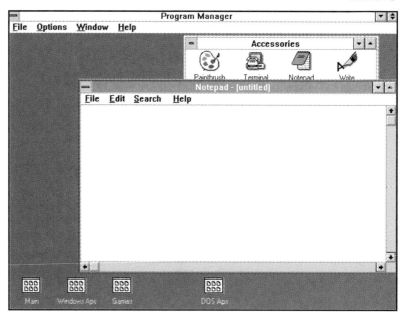

Oops!
You cannot delete a notepad file through the Notepad accessory. To do so, you must use the File Manager. See *TASK: Delete a file.*

1. **Start the Notepad accessory.**

   You use the Notepad accessory to enter notes. This program is stored in the Accessories group window. To start Notepad, double-click on the Accessories group icon. Then double-click on the Notepad icon. (This icon looks like a notepad.) For information on this step, see *TASK: Run a program.*

   You see a blank window. The title bar displays Notepad, followed by Untitled. Below the title bar you see the menu bar for Notepad. The mouse pointer is inside the blank area of the window, which is where you enter text.

2. **Type TO DO LIST.**

   TO DO LIST is the note's title, and it reminds you of the note's contents.

3. **Press Enter twice.**

   Pressing Enter twice ends the current line, inserts a blank line, and moves the mouse pointer to the next line.

4. **Type Get results from sales survey.**

   This is the text of the note. You can enter up to 50,000 characters in a note. You shouldn't have to worry about hitting this limit!

   Next you save the notepad file.

5. **Click on File in the menu bar.**

   This step opens the File menu. You see a list of File commands.

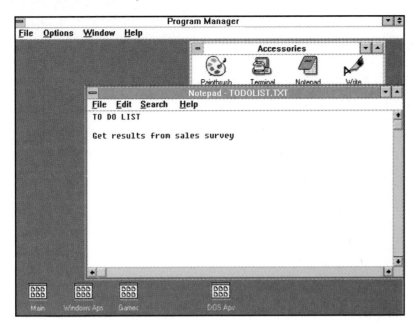

after

6. Click on **Save**.

This step selects the Save command and displays the File Save As dialog box. Inside this box, you see a Filename text box. (The mouse pointer is positioned inside this box.) The current directory and a list of directories are also listed in the dialog box.

7. Type **TODOLIST**.

TODOLIST is the name of the notepad file. The file is saved automatically with a TXT (indicating text) extension.

8. Press **Enter**.

Pressing Enter confirms the name and saves the file. You still see the note on-screen. The name of the note appears in the title bar.

Close Notepad
To close Notepad, double-click on the Control menu box for this window.

Save the note again
After you have saved a file for the first time, simply click on File and then select Save to save the file again. The file is saved with the same name.

REVIEW

To create a note

1. Start the **Notepad** accessory.

2. Type the text for the note.

3. Click on the **File** menu.

4. Click on **Save**.

5. Type a file name.

6. Press **Enter**.

Open a note

before

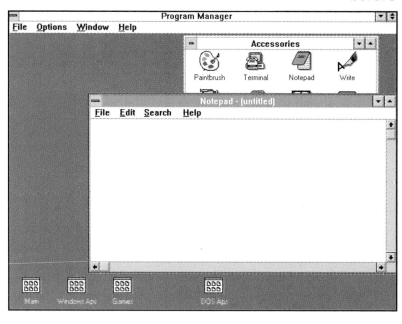

Oops!
To close Notepad, save the note and then double-click on the Control menu box for that window.

1. **Start the Notepad accessory.**

   To start Notepad, double-click on the Accessories group icon. Then double-click on the Notepad icon. For information on this step, see *TASK: Run a program*.

   On-screen you see a blank note window.

2. **Click on File in the menu bar.**

   This step opens the File menu. You see a list of File commands.

3. **Click on Open.**

   This step selects the Open command. You see the File Open dialog box. This dialog box includes a Filename text box. (The mouse pointer is positioned inside this box.) The current directory is also listed in the dialog box, and you see a Files list and a Directory list.

4. **Type TODOLIST.**

   TODOLIST is the name of the file that you want to open. You can also select the file by pointing to it in the Files list box and clicking the mouse button.

5. **Press Enter.**

   Pressing Enter confirms the file name; the note appears on-screen.

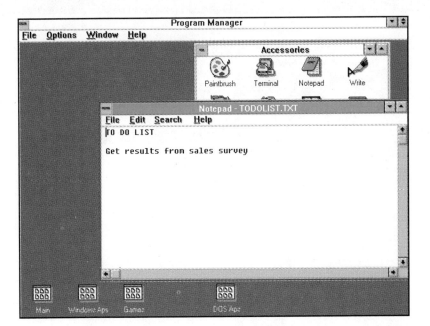

after

Try a shortcut
You can select and open a file by double-clicking on the file name in the Files list.

REVIEW

1. Start the **Notepad** accessory.

2. Click on **File** in the menu bar.

3. Click on the **Open** command.

4. Type the name of the file that you want to open.

5. Press **Enter**.

To open a note

Edit a note

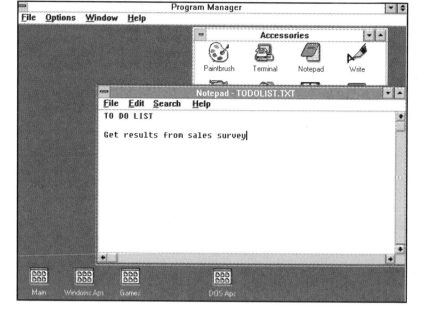

Oops!
If you change your mind about the editing changes, don't save the note.

1. **Start the Notepad accessory.**

   To start Notepad, double-click on the Accessories group icon. Then double-click on the Notepad icon. For information on this step, see *TASK: Run a program*.

2. **Open the TODOLIST note.**

   If you don't have a note named TODOLIST, open one that you do have. See *TASK: Open a note* for more information on this step.

3. **Click after the *y* in *survey*.**

   The *y* marks the end of the current note, and you want to begin editing here.

4. **Press Enter.**

   Pressing Enter ends the line and moves the mouse pointer to the next line.

5. **Type Finish marketing report.**

   Typing this text adds to the current note.

6. **Click on File and then Save.**

   This step opens the File menu and selects the Save command. The new note is saved to disk and replaces the previous version of the note.

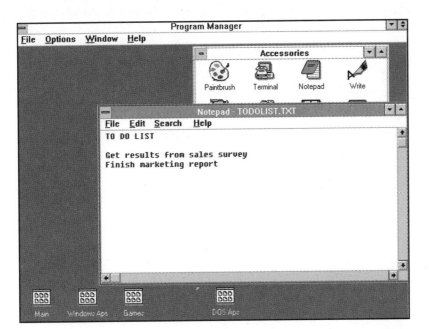

after

Can't find the note?
Remember that the Notepad always opens with a new, blank window. From this screen, you open the note that you want.

1. Start the **Notepad** accessory.

2. Open the note that you want to edit.

3. Make any editing changes.

4. Click on **File** and then **Save** to save the note.

To edit a note

Print a note

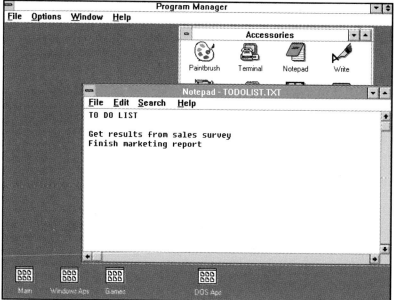

Oops!
While the document is printing, you see a dialog box on-screen. Click on Cancel to stop printing.

1. **Start the Notepad accessory.**

   To start Notepad, double-click on the Accessories group icon. Then double-click on the Notepad icon. For information on this step, see *TASK: Run a program*.

2. **Open the TODOLIST file.**

   TODOLIST is the file that you want to print. If you do not have a file named TODOLIST, open a file that you do have. See *TASK: Open a note* for more information on this step.

3. **Click on File in the menu bar.**

   This step opens the File menu. You see a list of File commands.

4. **Click on Print.**

   This step selects the Print command. The note is sent to the printer, which then prints you a paper copy.

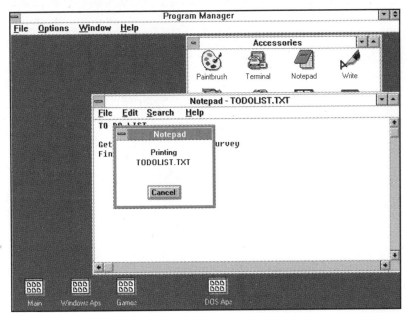

after

Note doesn't print?
If the note does not print, check to be sure that you have selected a printer. For more information on printer setup, see *Using Microsoft Windows 3*, 2nd Edition.

1. Start the **Notepad** accessory.

2. Open the note that you want to print.

3. Click on **File** in the menu bar.

4. Click on the **Print** command.

To print a note

Close Notepad
To close Notepad, save the note and then double-click on the Control menu box for the Notepad window.

Accessory Programs

133

Create a cardfile

Oops!
To delete a card, see
TASK: Delete a card.

before

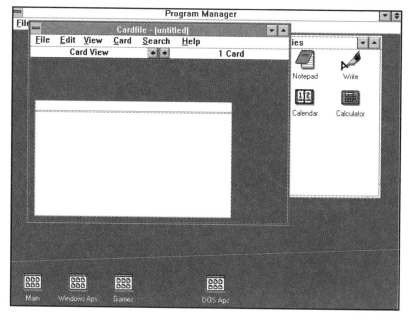

1. **Start the Cardfile accessory.**

   To enter cards, you use the Cardfile accessory. This program is stored in the Accessories program group. To open the Cardfile group window, double-click on the Accessories icon. Then double-click on the Cardfile icon. (This icon looks like a Rolodex.) For information on this step, see *TASK: Run a program.*

   You see a blank card on-screen. The names of the accessory (Cardfile) and the cardfile (untitled) appear in the title bar. Below the title bar you see the available menu options.

   A cardfile is a collection of cards; all the cards are stored together as one unit. When you want to edit or create new cards, you must first open the cardfile. See *TASK: Open a cardfile.*

2. **Type McDaniel, Millie.**

   McDaniel, Millie is the text for the first line of the card.

3. **Press Enter.**

   Pressing Enter ends the line and moves the mouse pointer to the next line.

4. **Type 5660 South Main Street.**

   This text is the address line. You can add more lines to the card.

   A card consists of two parts: the text and the index line. Microsoft Windows uses the index line to sort the card. For the first card that you create, you add the text and then the index line. For other cards, you add the index line first. (See *TASK: Add cards.*)

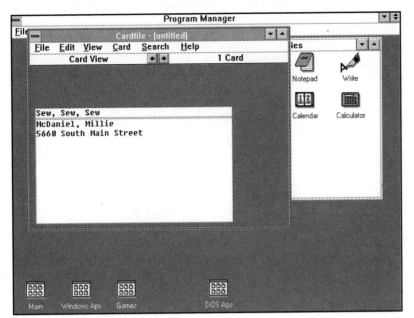

after

Save a cardfile
When you finish adding cards, you need to save the cardfile. See *TASK: Save a cardfile*.

5. Click on **Edit** in the menu bar.

    This step opens the Edit menu. You see a list of Edit commands.

6. Click on **Index**.

    This step selects the Index command and displays the Index Line dialog box. The mouse pointer is positioned inside the Index Line text box.

Close Cardfile
To close Cardfile, save it and then double-click on the Control menu box for that window.

7. Type **Sew, Sew, Sew**.

    This text is the name of the company and the line that Microsoft Windows uses to sort the entry. It is called the *index line*.

8. Press **Enter**.

    Pressing Enter completes entering the index line. The text appears at the top of the card, and it is separated from the card text by a double line.

REVIEW

1. Start the **Cardfile** accessory.

2. Type the text of the card.

3. Click on **Edit** in the menu bar.

4. Click on the **Index** command.

5. Type the index line for the card and press **Enter**.

To create a cardfile

Save a cardfile

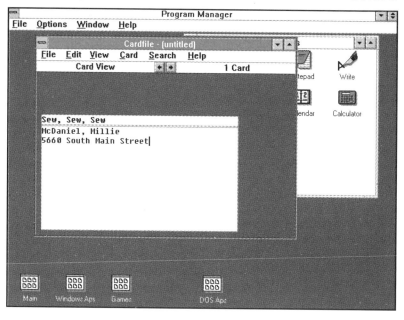

1. **Start the Cardfile accessory.**

   To open the Cardfile accessory, double-click on the Accessories icon. Then double-click on the Cardfile icon. (This icon looks like a Rolodex.) For information on this step, see *TASK: Run a program*.

2. **Create a cardfile and enter cards.**

   See *TASK: Create a cardfile* and *TASK: Add cards* for more information on this step.

3. **Click on File in the menu bar.**

   This step opens the File menu. You see a list of File commands.

4. **Click on Save.**

   This step selects the Save command and displays the File Save As dialog box. Inside this box, you see a Filename text box. (The mouse pointer is positioned inside this box.) The current directory and a list of directories are also listed in the dialog box.

5. **Type SHOPS.**

   SHOPS is the name that you want to assign to the cardfile. The name can be up to eight characters long and cannot contain any spaces. As a general rule, use only alphanumeric characters.

6. **Press Enter.**

   Pressing Enter saves the file. The file is saved with the extension CRD. The card remains on-screen, and the name of the cardfile appears in the title bar.

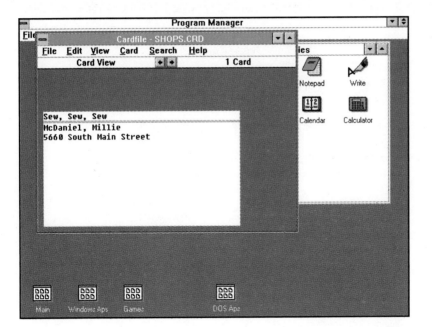

after

Save again
After you have saved a file once, you can click on File and then Save to save the file again. The file is saved with the same name.

REVIEW

1. Open the **Cardfile** accessory.

2. Create a cardfile and enter the card(s).

3. Click on **File** in the menu bar.

4. Click on the **Save** command.

5. If you have not saved the file already, type a file name.

6. Press **Enter**.

To save a cardfile

Open a cardfile

before

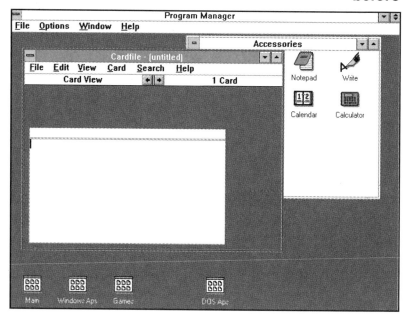

1. **Start the Cardfile accessory.**

    To open the Cardfile accessory, double-click on the Accessories icon. Then double-click on the Cardfile icon. For information on this step, see *TASK: Run a program*.

    To review, edit, or add cards, you must open the cardfile.

2. **Click on File in the menu bar.**

    This step opens the File menu. You see a list of File commands.

3. **Click on Open.**

    This step selects the Open command. You see the File Open dialog box. This dialog box includes a Filename text box. (The mouse pointer is positioned in this text box.) The current directory is also listed in the dialog box, and you see a files list and a directory list.

4. **Type SHOPS.**

    SHOPS is the name of the cardfile that you want to open. If you don't have a file named SHOPS, type the name of one that you do have. You can also point to the file name in the Files list box and click the mouse button to select the file.

5. **Press Enter.**

    Pressing Enter confirms the file name. You see the first card in the cardfile.

    As a shortcut, you can double-click on the file name in the Files list to select and open the file.

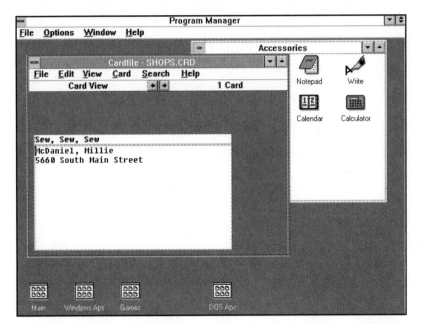

after

Close the Cardfile
To close Cardfile, save the cardfile and then double-click on the Control menu box for the Cardfile window.

REVIEW

1. Start the **Cardfile** accessory.

2. Click on **File** in the menu bar.

3. Click on the **Open** command.

4. Type the name of the file that you want to open.

5. Press **Enter**.

To open a cardfile

Scroll through cards
To scroll to other cards, click on the scroll arrows that are located under the menu.

Add cards

before

Program Manager

File Options Window Help

Accessories

Cardfile - SHOPS.CRD

File Edit View Card Search Help

Card View   1 Card

Sew, Sew, Sew
McDaniel, Millie
5660 South Main Street

Notepad   Write

Calendar   Calculator

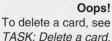

Main   Windows Aps   Games   DOS Aps

Oops!
To delete a card, see
TASK: Delete a card.

1. Start the **Cardfile** accessory.

   To open the Cardfile accessory, double-click on the Accessories icon. Then double-click on the Cardfile icon.

2. Open the **SHOPS** cardfile.

   For information on this step, see *TASK: Open a cardfile.* You see the first card on-screen.

3. Click on **Card** in the menu.

   This step opens the Card menu.

4. Click on **Add**.

   This step selects the Add command. The Add dialog box appears on-screen. When you create the first card, you enter the card text and then the index line. With new cards, you must enter the index line first. You enter the index line in the Add dialog box.

5. Type **Country Crafts**.

   Country Crafts is the index line for the card. The card is sorted by its index line.

6. Press **Enter**.

   Pressing Enter confirms the index line and creates a new card.

7. Type **Ball, Darlene**.

   This text is the name of the shop owner.

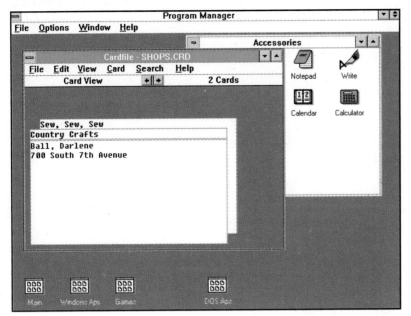

after

8. **Press Enter.**

   Pressing Enter ends the line and moves the mouse pointer to the next line.

9. **Type 700 South 7th Avenue.**

   This text is the address line.

10. **Click on File and then Save.**

    This step opens the File menu, selects the Save command, and saves the file.

Use a consistent format
Use the same format for new cards that you did for the first card that you created. This keeps the information better organized.

REVIEW

To add cards

1. Open the **Cardfile** accessory.

2. Open the cardfile that you want to use.

3. Click on **Card**.

4. Click on **Add**.

5. Type the index line for the card and press **Enter**.

6. Type the text of the card.

7. Click on **File** and then **Save** to save the cardfile.

Edit a card

before

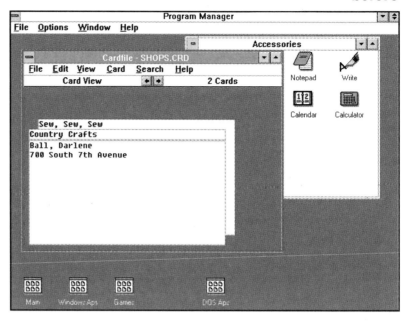

Oops!
If you see a blank card when you start, don't worry. Your cards are not missing. To find your cards, you must open the cardfile.

1. **Start the Cardfile accessory.**

   To open the Cardfile accessory, double-click on the Accessories icon. Then double-click on the Cardfile icon. For information on this step, see *TASK: Run a program*.

2. **Open the SHOPS cardfile.**

   The SHOPS cardfile contains the card you want to edit. See *TASK: Open a cardfile* for more information. You see the Country Crafts card on-screen, which is the first card—alphabetically—of the cards that you have entered.

3. **Press the PgDn key.**

   Pressing the PgDn key displays the next card. You want the card titled *Sew, Sew, Sew*.

   (If you have not created the cards for other cardfile tasks, you will not find this card. Find one that you do have.)

4. **Click after the *t* in *Street*.**

   This step positions the mouse pointer at the location where you want to add new text.

5. **Press Enter.**

   Pressing Enter ends the line and moves the mouse pointer to the next line.

6. **Type Dolls, jumpers, quilts.**

   This new text is added to the card.

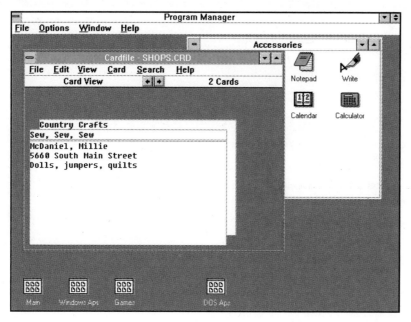

after

7. Click on **File** and then **Save**.
   This step opens the File menu, selects the Save command, and
   saves the cardfile.

To edit a card

1. Start the **Cardfile** accessory.

2. Open the cardfile that contains the card you want to
   edit.

3. Use the scroll arrows to move to the card. Or press the
   PgDn or PgUp key to move to the card.

4. Click next to the line that you want to edit.

5. Make any changes.

6. Click on **File** and then **Save** to save the appointment
   file.

Find a card

before

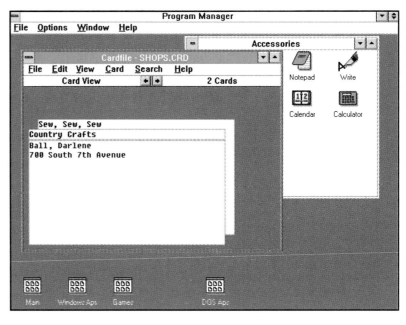

1. **Start the Cardfile accessory.**

   To open the Cardfile accessory, double-click on the Accessories icon. Then double-click on the Cardfile icon. For information on this step, see *TASK: Run a program.*

2. **Open the SHOPS cardfile.**

   The SHOPS cardfile contains the card that you want to find. See *TASK: Open cardfile* for more information.

3. **Click on Search in the menu bar.**

   This step opens the Search menu.

4. **Click on Find.**

   This step selects the Find command. You see the Find dialog box. (The mouse pointer is positioned inside this text box.)

5. **Type quilts.**

   Quilts is the text that you want to find. (Note that if you didn't add this text to the card in *TASK: Edit a card*, you will not be able to find it now. If so, search for text on a card that you do have.)

6. **Press Enter.**

   Pressing Enter starts the search. Microsoft Windows moves to the first card that contains *quilt*. This is the card for Sew, Sew, Sew.

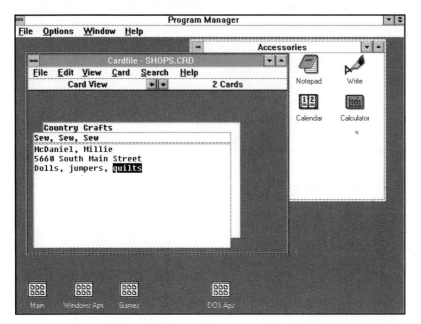

after

If a match isn't found...
If no match is found, you
see an alert box that says
Cannot find *text*.
(The word *text* is replaced
by the text for which you
were searching.)

REVIEW

1. Start the **Cardfile** accessory.

2. Open the cardfile that contains the card you want to find.

3. Click on **Search** in the menu bar.

4. Click on the **Find** command.

5. Type the text for which you want to search.

6. Press **Enter**.

To find a card

Search again
To find the next match,
click on Search and then
click on File Next. Notice
that Find does not search
the index line.

Print all cards

before

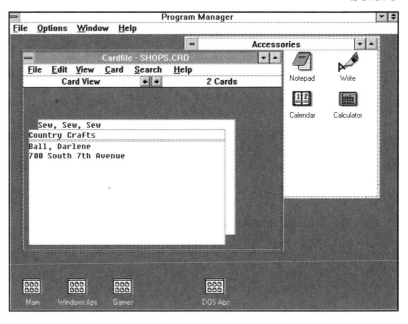

Oops!
While Microsoft Windows is printing, you see a dialog box on-screen that contains a Cancel button. Click on Cancel to stop printing.

1. **Start the Cardfile accessory.**

   To open the Cardfile group window, double-click on the Accessories icon. Then double-click on the Cardfile icon to start the program. For information on this step, see *TASK: Run a program*.

2. **Open the SHOPS file.**

   You will print all the cards in the SHOPS file. See *TASK: Open a cardfile* for more information on this step. If you do not have this cardfile, open one that you do have.

3. **Click on File in the menu bar.**

   This step opens the File menu. You see a list of File commands.

4. **Click on Print All.**

   This step selects the Print All command. All cards are printed.

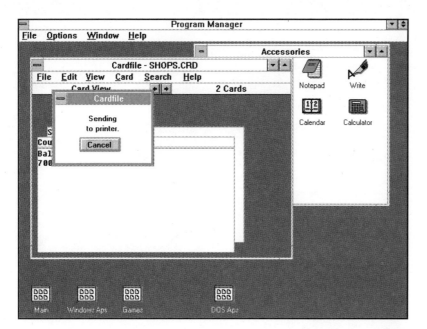

after

The cards don't print?
If the cards do not print, make sure that you have selected a printer. For more information, see *Using Microsoft Windows 3*, 2nd Edition.

REVIEW

1. Start the **Cardfile** accessory.

2. Open the cardfile that you want to print.

3. Click on **File** in the menu bar.

4. Click on the **Print All** command.

To print all cards

Delete a card

before

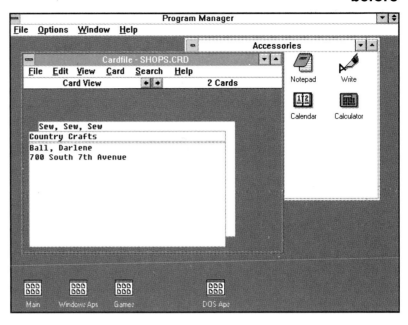

Oops!
If you decide that you do not want to delete the card, click on Cancel in the alert box that appears.

1. **Start the Cardfile accessory.**

   To start the Cardfile accessory, double-click on the Accessories icon. Then double-click on the Cardfile icon. For information on this step, see *TASK: Run a program*.

2. **Open the SHOPS cardfile.**

   The SHOPS cardfile contains the file that you want to delete. See *TASK: Open a cardfile* for more information. If you don't have this cardfile, open one that you do have.

   The first card in the stack, Country Crafts, is displayed. You want to delete this card. If this card isn't displayed, use the scroll arrows below the menu bar to scroll to the card.

3. **Click on Card in the menu bar.**

   This step opens the Card menu.

4. **Click on Delete.**

   This step selects the Delete command. You see an alert box that says Delete "Country Crafts"?.

5. **Click on OK.**

   This step confirms the deletion. The card is deleted.

6. **Click on File and then Save.**

   This step opens the File menu, selects the Save command, and saves the cardfile.

Easy **Windows**

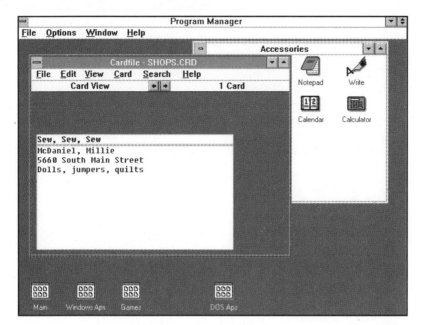

after

Open the correct file
If you see a blank card when you start, don't worry. Your cards are not missing. To find your cards, you must open the cardfile.

To delete a card

1. Start the **Cardfile** accessory.

2. Open the cardfile that contains the card you want to delete.

3. Use the scroll arrows or the PgDn and PgUp key to move to the card that you want to delete.

4. Click on **Card** in the menu bar.

5. Click on the **Delete** command.

6. Click on **OK**.

7. Click on **File** and then **Save** to save the cardfile.

Start Windows Write

before

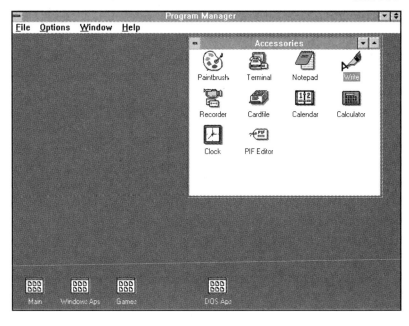

1. **Double-click on the Accessories icon.**

   The Write program is stored in the Accessories program group. To start the program, you open the window for that group.

   On-screen, you see several icons in a window. The icon for Write looks like a pen stylus.

2. **Double-click on the Write icon.**

   This step opens the Write program. You see a blank document on-screen. The title bar reminds you of the name of the program (Write) and the document (Untitled). The document remains untitled until you save it.

   Notice that Write is a word processing program with its own menu system and help. The program offers many editing and formatting features. This book covers some basic tasks—creating, saving, opening, editing, and printing a document. Including all Write features, however, is beyond the scope of this book. You might want to experiment with what you already know about Microsoft Windows and Microsoft Windows programs. For complete information about the Write program, see *Using Microsoft Windows 3,* 2nd Edition.

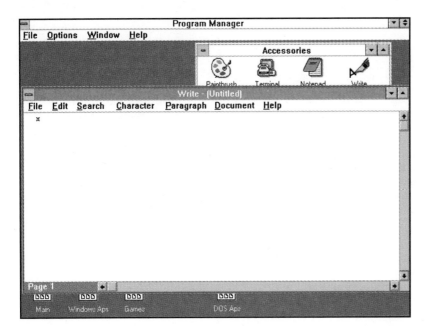

after

Maximize a window
To see more of the Write screen, maximize the window. See *TASK: Maximize a window.*

REVIEW

1. Double-click on the **Accessories** icon.

2. Double-click on the **Write** icon.

To start Windows Write

Create a Write document

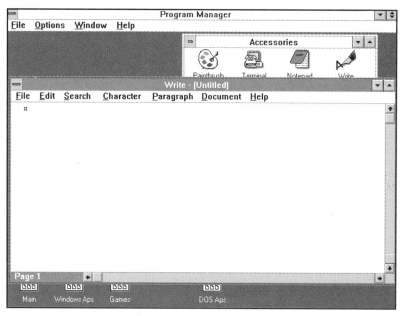

Oops!
To close the document without saving it, click on File and then Exit. When prompted to save the current changes, click on No.

1. **Start the Write program.**

   For information on this task, see *TASK: Start Windows Write*. You see a blank document. The mouse pointer is blinking on-screen.

2. **Type MEMO.**

   MEMO is the first line of the new document.

3. **Press Enter twice.**

   Pressing Enter twice ends the line, moves the mouse pointer to the beginning of the next line, and inserts a blank line.

4. **Type Don't forget that Friday, June 7 is a special company holiday. The office will be closed this day so that we can have a company picnic.**

   As you type, the mouse pointer moves right. When you reach the end of the line, the text automatically moves (or wraps) to the next line. You do not have to press Enter to end a line.

5. **Press Enter twice.**

   Pressing Enter twice ends the line, moves the mouse pointer to the beginning of the next line, and inserts a blank line.

6. **Type See you at Sahm park for the annual picnic.**

   This step completes the text of the document. Remember that Write offers many more features than this simple exercise shows. You can copy text, move text, make text bold, and perform many other editing and formatting tasks. For complete information, see *Using Microsoft Windows 3,* 2nd Edition.

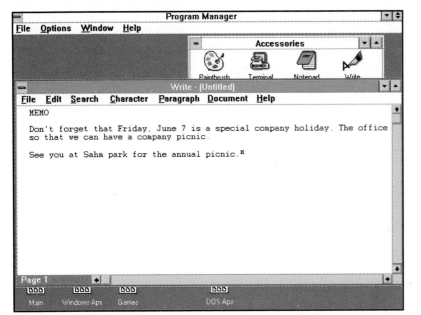

after

1. Start the **Write** program.

2. Type the text.

**See something
different?**
Depending on your printer
and the typefaces that
you have selected, your
lines may break
differently than those in
the After screen.

To create a Write document

Typeface not right?
If the text does not
appear clearly (the text is
not sharp), you should
select a different
typeface. See *Using
Microsoft Windows 3,* 2nd
Edition for more
information.

Save a Write document

before

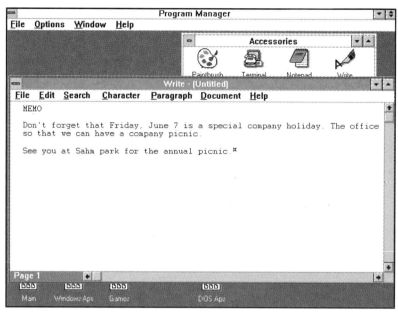

Oops!
Be sure to save the file before you close the program. If you don't save, Microsoft Windows prompts you to do so.

1. Start the **Write** program.

   For information on this step, see *TASK: Start Windows Write.*

2. Create a document.

   See *TASK: Create a Write document* for help with this step.

3. Click on the **File** menu.

   This step opens the File menu. You see a list of File commands.

4. Click on **Save**.

   This step selects the Save command and displays the File Save As dialog box. Inside this box, you see a Filename text box. (The mouse pointer is positioned inside this box.) The current directory and a list of directories also are listed in the dialog box.

5. Type **MEMO**.

   MEMO is the name that you want to assign the document. The document name can be up to eight characters long and cannot have any spaces. As a general rule, use only alphanumeric characters.

6. Press **Enter**.

   Pressing Enter saves the file. The file is saved with the extension WRI. The file remains on-screen, and the name appears in the title bar.

   To open a file that you have saved, see *TASK: Open a Write document.* To clear the current document and create a new document, click on File and then New.

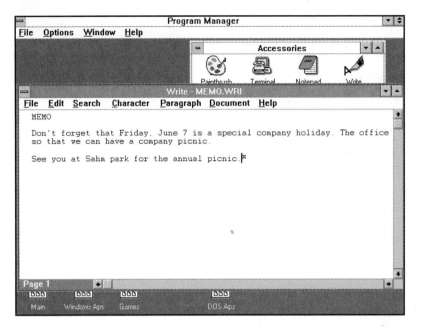

after

Already created a document?
If you have created the document already, skip steps 1 and 2. Start with step 3.

1. Open the **Write** program.

2. Create a document.

3. Click on the **Save** command.

4. If you have not saved the file already, type a file name.

5. Press **Enter**.

To save a Write document

Save a document again
After you have saved a file for the first time, click on File and then Save to save the file again. The updated file is saved with the same name.

Open a Write document

before

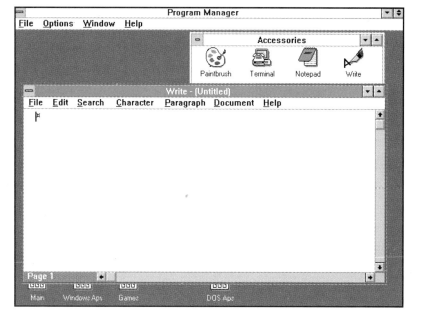

Oops!

To close the Write program, save the document and then double-click on the Control menu box for the Write window.

1. **Start the Write program.**

   For information on this step, see *TASK: Start Windows Write.*

2. **Click on File.**

   This step opens the File menu. You see a list of File commands.

3. **Click on Open.**

   This step selects the Open command. You see the File Open dialog box. This dialog box includes a Filename text box. (The mouse pointer is positioned inside this text box.) The current directory also is listed in the dialog box. You see a Files list and a Directory list.

4. **Type MEMO.**

   MEMO is the name of the file you want to open. You can also point to the file name in the Files list box and click the mouse button to select the file.

5. **Press Enter.**

   Pressing Enter confirms the file name. You see the document on-screen. You now can make any editing or formatting changes. To save the document, click on File and then Save.

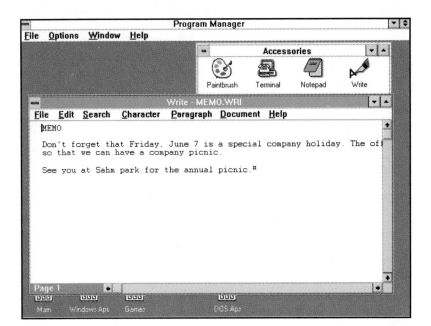

after

Try a shortcut
You can also select and open a file by double-clicking on the file name in the Files list box.

1. Start the Write program.

2. Click on File to open the File menu.

3. Click on Open to select the Open command.

4. Type the name of the file that you want to open.

5. Press Enter.

To open a Write document

Edit a Write document

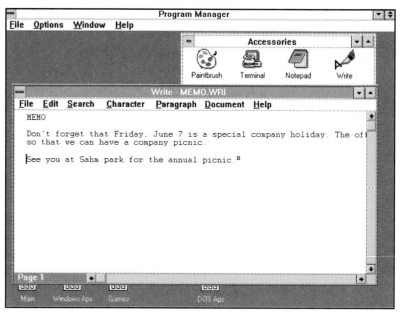

Oops!
If you don't like the edited document, don't save the changes.

1. Start the **Write** program.

   For information on this step, see *TASK: Start Windows Write.*

2. Open the **MEMO** document file.

   For help with this step, see *TASK: Open a Write document.* You see the document on-screen.

   If you have not created this document, open a document that you have created.

3. Click after the last sentence.

   This step positions the mouse pointer at the location where you want to insert text. The last sentence of the MEMO document that you created previously is *See you at Sahm park for the annual picnic.*

4. Press **Enter twice**.

   Pressing Enter twice ends the current line, inserts a blank line, and moves the mouse pointer to the beginning of the next line.

5. Type **Remember that it's a pitch in. Here are some suggestions on what to bring:**.

6. Press **Enter twice**.

   Pressing Enter twice ends the current line, inserts a blank line, and moves the mouse pointer to the beginning of the next line.

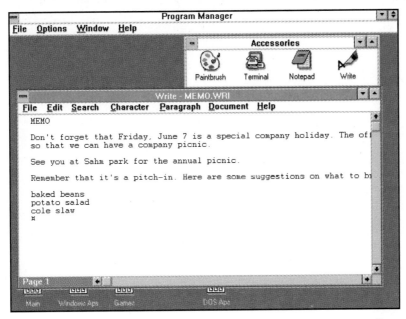

after

7. Type the following items, pressing Enter after each one:

   baked beans

   potato salad

   cole slaw

8. Save the document.

   For help with this step, see *TASK: Save a Write document*.

1. Start the **Write** program.

2. Click on **File** and then **Open** to select the File Open command.

3. Type the name of the file that you want to edit.

4. Make any editing changes.

5. Click on **File** and then **Save** to save the changes.

To edit a Write document

Cut and paste text

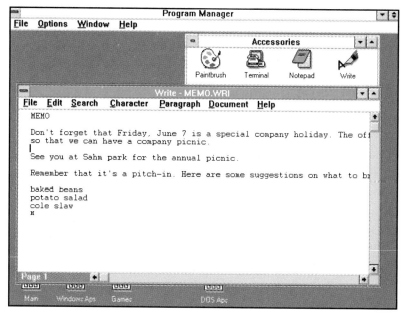

1. Start the **Write** program.

   For information on this step, see *TASK: Start Windows Write*.

2. Open the **MEMO** document file.

   For help with this step, see *TASK: Open a Write document*. You see the document on-screen.

   If you have not created this document, open a document that you have created.

3. Click on the blank line before the sentence that begins with the words *See you at*.

   This step positions the mouse pointer at the beginning of the text that you want to cut.

4. Press and hold the mouse button, then drag the mouse until you highlight the entire sentence, ending with the period.

   This step highlights the section of text that you want to cut. Be sure that you include the blank line preceding the sentence.

5. Click on **Edit** in the menu bar.

   This step opens the Edit menu. You see a list of Edit commands.

6. Click on **Cut**.

   This step selects the Cut command. The text is cut (removed) from the document and stored in a temporary holding place called the *clipboard*.

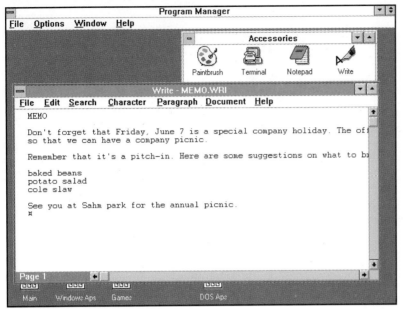

after

Be careful!
Be sure not to cut anything else before you paste. If you cut or copy other text, the new text replaces the original text in the clipboard.

7. **Click on the blank line after *cole slaw*.**

   This is the place where you want to insert the cut text.

8. **Click on Edit in the menu bar.**

   This step opens the Edit menu.

9. **Click on Paste.**

   This step selects the Paste command and pastes (inserts) the cut text at the mouse pointer location.

10. **Save the document.**

    For help with this step, see *TASK: Save a Write document*.

Cut and paste options
You can cut and paste data between documents and between different programs. See *Using Microsoft Windows 3, 2nd Edition*.

REVIEW

1. Select the text that you want to cut.

2. Click on **Edit** in the menu bar.

3. Click on the **Cut** command.

4. Move the mouse pointer to the location where you want the text to appear.

5. Click on **Edit** in the menu bar.

6. Click on **Paste**.

To cut and paste text

Center text

before

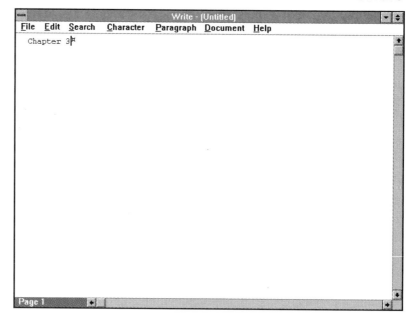

Oops!
To return to left alignment, select Paragraph Left.

1. **Start the Write program.**

   For information on this task, see *TASK: Start Windows Write*. You see a blank document. The mouse pointer is blinking on-screen.

2. **Click the Maximize button.**

   The Maximize button is the up arrow in the right corner of the title bar. This step enlarges the document window so that it fills the entire screen.

3. **Type Chapter 3.**

   Chapter 3 is the text that you want to center.

4. **Click on Paragraph in the menu bar.**

   This step opens the Paragraph menu.

5. **Click on Centered.**

   This step selects the Centered command. The text is centered on-screen.

6. **Press Enter.**

   Pressing Enter moves the cursor to the next paragraph and ensures that the next paragraph will also be centered. You can tell this because the cursor position remains in the center of the line when it moves down a line.

7. **Click on Paragraph in the menu bar.**

   This step opens the Paragraph menu.

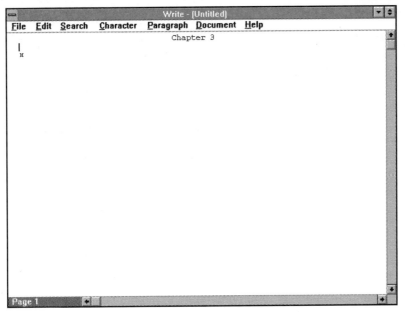

after

Center before
or after typing
You can center text
before or after you type it.
To center text before,
select the command and
then type the text.

8. Click on **Left**.

   This step selects left alignment and returns the cursor to the left margin. The text that you type next will be aligned with the left margin, not centered.

9. Save the document.

   See *TASK: Save a Write document* for help with this step. Name the document *CHAP3*.

1. Type the text.

2. Click on **Paragraph** in the menu bar.

3. Click on the **Centered** command.

To center text

Make text bold

before

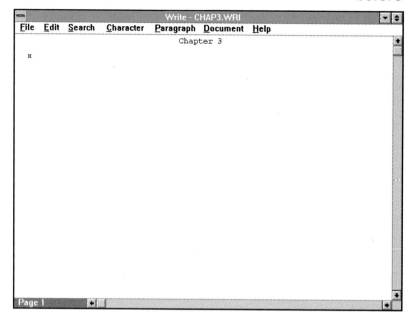

Oops!
To turn off bold, select the Character Normal command.

1. **Start the Write program.**

   For information on this task, see *TASK: Start Windows Write*. You see a blank document. The mouse pointer is blinking on-screen.

2. **Click the Maximize button.**

   The Maximize button is the up arrow in the right corner of the title bar. This step enlarges the document window so that it fills the entire screen.

3. **Open the CHAP3 document file.**

   For help with this step, see *TASK: Open a Write document*. The document appears on-screen. If you do not have a CHAP3 document, open one that you do have.

4. **Click before the *C* in *Chapter*.**

   This step places the cursor in the correct position so that you can select the text that you want.

5. **Press and hold the mouse button and drag the mouse until you highlight Chapter 3.**

   This step selects the text that you want to make bold.

6. **Click on Character in the menu bar.**

   This step opens the Character menu.

Easy **Windows**

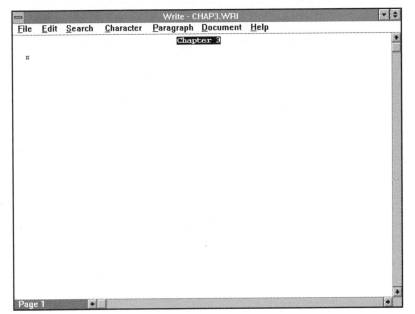

after

7. Click on **Bold**.

    This step selects the Bold command. The text remains selected on-screen. It appears in boldface. You can follow this same procedure to make other text enhancements, such as italic, underline, and so on. See *Using Windows 3*, Second Edition, for more information.

1. Select the text that you want to make bold.

2. Click on **Character** in the menu bar.

3. Click on **Bold**.

**Specify bold
before you type**
You can also specify boldface before you type. Simply select the Character Bold command, type the text you want to be bold, and then select the Character Normal command.

To make text bold

Try a shortcut
You can also use the Ctrl-B key combination to select the Character Bold command.

Indent text

before

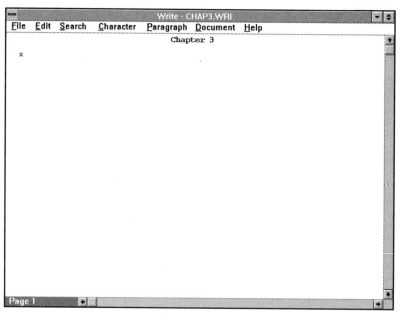

1. **Start the Write program.**

   For information on this task, see *TASK: Start Windows Write*. You see a blank document. The mouse pointer is blinking on-screen.

2. **Click the Maximize button.**

   The Maximize button is the up arrow in the right corner of the title bar. This step enlarges the document window so that it fills the entire screen.

3. **Open the CHAP3 document file.**

   For help with this step, see *TASK: Open a Write document*. The document appears on-screen. If you do not have a CHAP3 document, open one that you do have.

4. **Click on the space before the end-of-file marker.**

   The end-of-file marker looks like a star and should be along the edge of the left margin. Clicking on the space just before this marker positions the cursor at the end of the text in the document.

5. **Press Enter.**

   Pressing Enter inserts a blank line between the chapter title and the text.

6. **Click on Paragraph in the menu bar.**

   This step opens the Paragraph menu.

7. **Click on Indents.**

   This step selects the Indents command. The Indents dialog box appears.

Easy **Windows**

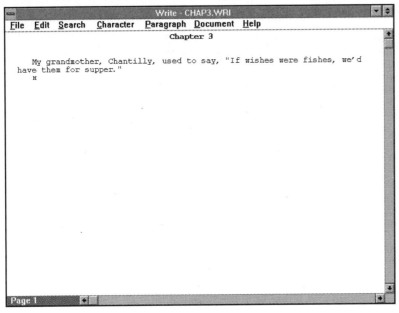

File Edit Search Character Paragraph Document Help

Chapter 3

My grandmother, Chantilly, used to say, "If wishes were fishes, we'd
have them for supper."

Page 1

after

8. **Press Tab**.

This step moves the cursor to the First Line text box. For this task, you specify a first line indent (all other lines will be flush left).

9. **Type .25**.

Typing *.25* sets the indent at one-quarter of an inch.

10. **Press Enter**.

Pressing Enter confirms the new setting. The cursor moves to the indent setting, which is one-quarter of an inch from the margin.

11. **Type My grandmother, Chantilly, used to say, "If wishes were fishes, we'd have them for supper."**

This is first paragraph of indented text in the document. Notice that the first line of this paragraph is indented, but the second line returns to the left margin.

REVIEW

To indent text

1. Click on Paragraph in the menu bar.

2. Click on **Indents**.

3. Type the values for the indents you want to set: Left Indent, First Line Indent, and Right Indent.

4. Press **Enter**.

5. Type the text.

Find text

before

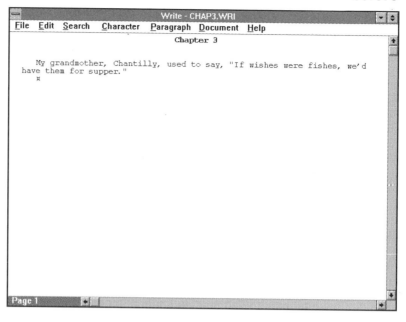

1. Start the **Write** program.

   For information on this task, see *TASK: Start Windows Write*. You see a blank document. The mouse pointer is blinking on-screen.

2. Click the **Maximize** button.

   The Maximize button is the up arrow in the right corner of the title bar. This step enlarges the document window so that it fills the entire screen.

3. Open the **CHAP3** document file.

   For help with this step, see *TASK: Open a Write document*. The document appears on-screen. If you do not have a CHAP3 document, open one that you do have.

4. Click on **Search** in the menu bar.

   This step opens the Search menu.

5. Click on **Find**.

   This step selects the Find command. The Find dialog box appears, and the cursor is positioned in the Find What text box.

6. Type **fishes**.

   This is the text that you want to find.

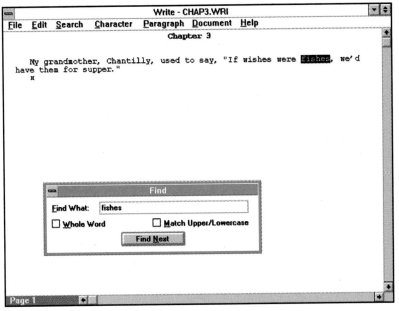

after

7. **Press Enter.**

    Pressing Enter starts the search. Write moves to the first occurrence of the text and selects it. The Find dialog box remains open on-screen. You can click Find Next to find the next occurrence or double-click the control icon to close the Find dialog box.

1. Click on **Search** in the menu bar.

2. Click on **Find**.

3. Type the text you want to find.

4. Press **Enter**.

5. Double-click the **Control menu box** to close the Find window. Or click **Find Next** to continue the search.

To find text

Print a Write document

before

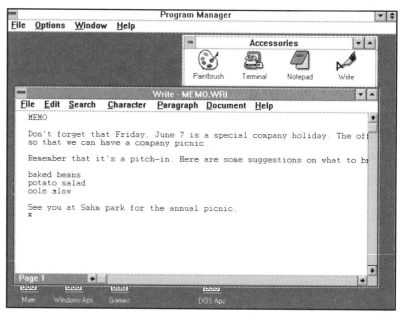

Oops!
While the document is printing, you see a dialog box on-screen. Click on Cancel to stop printing.

1. Start the **Write** program.

   For information on this step, see *TASK: Start Windows Write*.

2. Open the **MEMO** file.

   For information on this step, see *TASK: Open a Write document*. If you have not created this document, open one that you have created.

3. Click on **File**.

   This step opens the File menu. You see a list of File commands.

4. Click on **Print**.

   This step selects the Print command. The Print dialog box appears on-screen. The mouse pointer is positioned inside the Copies text box.

5. Press **Enter**.

   Pressing Enter tells Write to print one copy of the document.

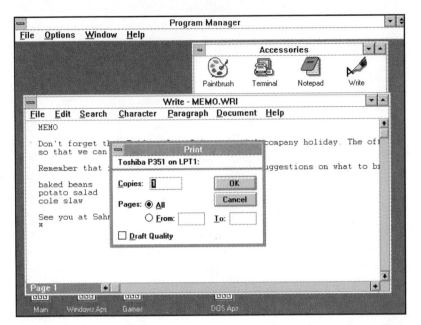

after

Nothing prints?
If the document does not print, make sure that you have selected a printer. See *Using Microsoft Windows 3,* 2nd Edition for more information.

REVIEW

1. Start the **Write** program.

2. Open the file that you want to print.

3. Click on **File** to open the File menu.

4. Click on **Print** to select the Print command.

5. Press **Enter** to print one copy.

To print a Write document

Start Windows Paintbrush

before

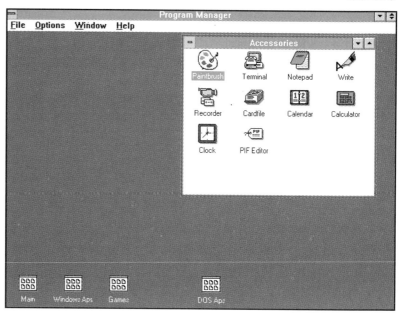

Oops!
To exit Paintbrush, double-click on the Control menu box for the Paintbrush window. If you have made any changes, you are prompted to save the drawing.

1. **Double-click on the Accessories icon.**

   The Paintbrush program is stored in the Accessories program group. To start the program, you open the window for that group.

   On-screen, you see several icons in a window. The icon for Paintbrush is a palette and brush.

2. **Double-click on the Paintbrush icon.**

   This step opens the Paintbrush program. You see a blank drawing area on-screen. The title bar reminds you of the name of the program (Paintbrush) and the drawing (Untitled). The drawing remains untitled until you save it.

   Along the top of the screen, you see the Paintbrush menu bar. Along the left side of the screen, you see icons for the Paintbrush tools. Along the bottom, you see the color selections.

   Notice that Paintbrush offers many paint features. Covering all Paintbrush features is beyond the scope of this book. You might want to experiment using what you already know about Microsoft Windows and Microsoft Windows programs. For additional information, see *Using Microsoft Windows 3, 2nd Edition*.

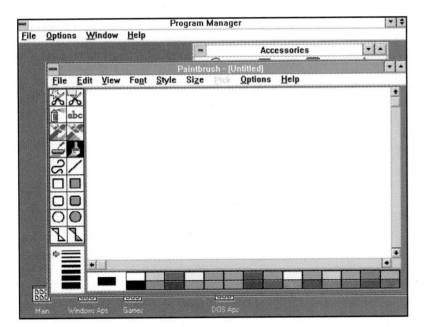

after

To see more of the
Paintbrush screen,
maximize the window.
See *TASK: Maximize a
window.*

REVIEW

1. Double-click on the **Accessories** icon.

2. Double-click on the **Paintbrush** icon.

To start Windows Paintbrush

Create a Paintbrush drawing

before

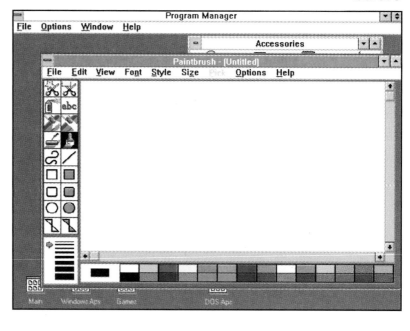

Oops!
If the circle doesn't appear as you want, click on Edit and then Undo to erase the circle.

1. Start the **Paintbrush** program.

   For information on this task, see *TASK: Start Windows Paintbrush*. A blank draw area appears on-screen.

2. Click on the **circle** tool.

   The Paintbrush tools are located along the left side of the window. The circle tool is in the first column near the bottom. Clicking on the tool selects the tool.

3. Move the mouse pointer into the middle of the draw area.

   When the mouse pointer is on the draw area, it turns into a crosshair.

4. Press and hold the mouse button and drag the mouse down and right until you have created a circle about three inches in diameter. Then release the mouse button.

   Use your best judgment to place and draw the circle. You should see a black circle on-screen.

5. Click on the **abc** tool in the toolbar.

   The abc tool is the text tool and appears in the second column near the top. This tool enables you to insert text.

6. Click on **Size** in the menu bar.

   This step displays a list of available font sizes.

after

7. Click on **48**.

   This step selects 48-point type, which is a large type size.

8. Position the mouse pointer just inside the left edge of the circle and click the left mouse button.

   Use your best judgment in placing the mouse pointer. To change the starting point, just click on the new spot.

9. Type **Ink, Inc.**

   This is the text for the logo. If the text doesn't fit, you can use Edit Undo to delete it. Then pick a smaller point size. Or start over and draw a bigger circle.

Start over
To start over, click on File and then New to clear the current drawing. When prompted to save the current image, click on No. A blank draw area appears.

Save the drawing
To save the drawing, see *TASK: Save a Paintbrush drawing.*

REVIEW

1. Start the **Paintbrush** program.

2. Use any of the draw tools to create a drawing.

To create a Paintbrush drawing

Save a Paintbrush drawing

Oops!
Be sure to save the file before you close the program. If you forget, you are prompted to save the changes.

1. **Start the Paintbrush program.**

   For information on this step, see *TASK: Start Windows Paintbrush*.

2. **Create the drawing.**

   For information on this step, see *TASK: Create a Paintbrush drawing*.

3. **Click on the File menu.**

   This step opens the File menu. You see a list of File commands.

4. **Click on Save.**

   This step selects the Save command and displays the File Save As dialog box. Inside this box, you see a Filename text box. (The mouse pointer is positioned inside this box.) The current directory and a list of directories also are listed.

5. **Type LOGO.**

   LOGO is the name that you want to assign the drawing.

6. **Press Enter.**

   Pressing the Enter key saves the file. The file is saved with the extension BMP. The drawing remains on-screen, and the name appears in the title bar.

after

Save again
After you have saved the file for the first time, simply click on File and then Save to save the file again. The file is saved with the same name.

1. Open the **Paintbrush** program.

2. Create a drawing.

3. Click on **Save**.

4. If you have not saved the file already, type a file name.

5. Press **Enter**.

To save a Paintbrush drawing

Try a shortcut
You can also press Ctrl-S to select the File Save command.

Open a Paintbrush drawing

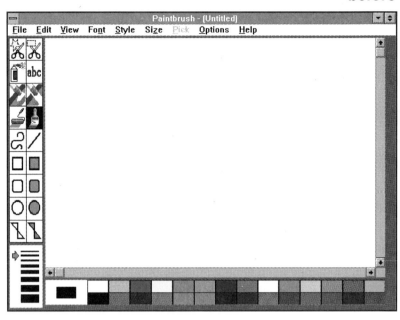

Oops!
To close the Paintbrush program, save the drawing and then double-click on the Control menu box for the Paintbrush window.

1. **Start the Paintbrush program.**

   For information on this task, see *TASK: Start Windows Paintbrush*. On-screen you see a blank draw area.

2. **Click the Maximize button.**

   The Maximize button is the up arrow in the right corner of the title bar. This step enlarges the document window so that it fills the entire screen.

3. **Click on File.**

   This step opens the File menu. A list of File commands appears.

4. **Click on Open.**

   This step selects the Open command. The File Open dialog box appears. This dialog box includes a Filename text box; the cursor is positioned inside this text box. The current directory is also listed in the dialog box, and you see two lists: a files list and a directory list.

5. **Type LOGO.**

   LOGO is the name of the file that you want to open. If you do not have a file named LOGO, select one that you do have. You can also point to the file name in the Files list box and click the mouse button to select the file.

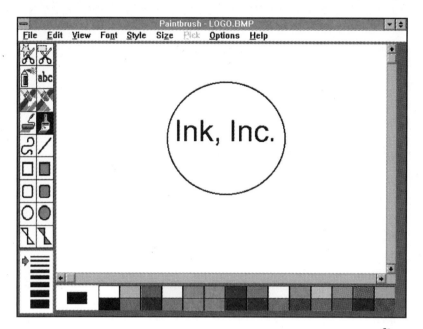

after

Try a shortcut
You can also select and open the file by double-clicking on the file name in the Files box.

6. **Press Enter**.

   Pressing the Enter key confirms the file name. You see the drawing on-screen. You can make any editing or formatting changes. To save the drawing, click on File and then Save.

REVIEW

1. Start the **Paintbrush** program.

2. Click on **File** to open the File menu.

3. Click on **Open** to select the Open command.

4. Type the name of the file you want to open.

5. Press **Enter**.

To open a Paintbrush drawing

Edit a drawing

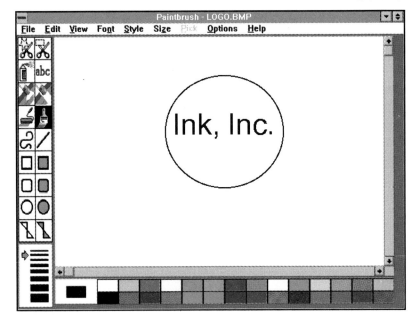

Oops!
If you don't like the color that you selected, simply follow these same steps and select a different color.

1. **Start the Paintbrush program.**

   For information on this task, see *TASK: Start Windows Paintbrush*. On-screen you see a blank draw area.

2. **Click the Maximize button.**

   The Maximize button is the up arrow in the right corner of the title bar. This step enlarges the document window so that it fills the entire screen.

3. **Open the LOGO document file.**

   For help with this step, see *TASK: Open a Write document*. The drawing appears on-screen. If you do not have a drawing called LOGO, open one that you do have.

4. **Click on the paint roller tool.**

   This tool is the fourth one in the first column. This tool fills an item with color.

5. **Click on light blue in the color bar along the bottom of the window.**

   Light blue is the sixth color in the top row. You can choose whatever color you want from the color bar.

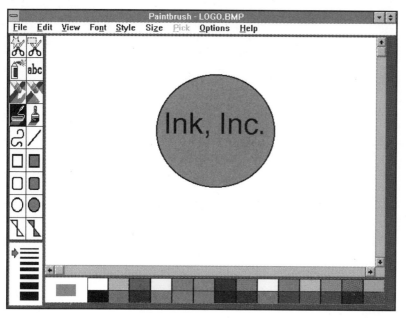

after

6. Click in the circle in the drawing.
   This step fills the circle with the selected color.

7. Click on **File** and then **Save**.
   This step saves the drawing.

1. Start the **Paintbrush** program.

2. Open the drawing that you want to edit.

3. Make any editing changes.

4. Save the drawing.

To edit a drawing

Reference

Quick Reference

Guide to Basic Keyboard Operations

Glossary

Easy **Windows**

Quick Reference

Task	Procedure
Select an icon	Click on the icon.
Select a window	Click on the window.
Open a window	Double-click on the window icon.
Start a program	Double-click on the program icon.
Quit a program	Double-click on the Control menu box.
Move a window	Click on the title bar, press and hold the mouse button, and drag the window to a new location. Release the mouse button.
Resize a window	Click on the title bar, press and hold the mouse button, and drag the borders to change the size. Release the mouse button.
Minimize a window	Click on the Minimize button.
Maximize a window	Click on the Maximize button.
Help	Click on Help in the menu bar.

Quit Windows	Double-click on the Control menu box of the Program Manager.
Select a file (File Manager)	Click on the file.
Select a directory (File Manager)	Click on the directory.
Select a drive (File Manager)	Click on the drive icon.
Collapse the selected directory (File Manager)	Click on the directory icon (the icon must have a minus sign).
Expand the selected directory (File Manager)	Click on the directory icon (the icon must have a plus sign).
Create directory (File Manager)	Select **File Create Directory**.
Search for file (File Manager)	Select **File Search**.
Copy file (File Manager)	Select **File Copy** or press the **F8** key.
Delete file (File Manager)	Select **File Delete** or press the **Del** key.
Rename file (File Manager)	Select **File Rename** or press the **F7** key.
Move file (File Manager)	Select **File Move**.
Format a disk (File Manager)	Select **Disk Format Diskette**.

Guide to Basic Keyboard Operations

Instead of using the mouse with Microsoft Windows, you can use the keyboard. This appendix covers some basic keyboard operations. For complete instructions on using the keyboard, see the Microsoft Windows manual or *Using Microsoft Windows 3*, 2nd Edition.

Open a menu

1. Press the **Alt** key to select the menu bar.
2. Use the ← or → key to move to the menu that you want to open.
3. Press **Enter**.

To open a menu quickly, press the **Alt** key and then type the underlined letter in the menu name.

Select a menu command

1. Open the menu.
2. Use the ↑ or ↓ key to move to the command that you want to open.
3. Press **Enter**.

To select a menu command quickly, type the underlined letter in the menu command name.

Select an option in a dialog box

Press and hold the Alt key; then type the underlined letter in the check box, text box, or list box.

Open the Control menu for an application window

Press the Alt key and then press the space bar.

Open the Control menu for other windows

Press the Alt key and then press the - (hyphen).

Glossary

application   A computer program that is used for a particular task such as word processing. In most cases, *program* and *application* mean the same thing and can be used interchangeably.

check box   A square box that appears in a dialog box. Check boxes can be checked (selected) or unchecked (unselected).

click   The action of pressing and releasing the mouse button.

clipboard   A temporary spot in memory that holds the text or graphics that you cut or copy.

close   To remove a window from the desktop.

command button   A choice of action that appears in a dialog box. Two common command buttons are OK and Cancel.

Control icon   The hyphen or little box that appears in the title bar of a window. Clicking on this box opens the Control menu. You use this menu to manipulate the window.

desktop   The screen background on which windows and icons are displayed.

dialog box   An on-screen window that displays further command options. Often, a dialog box reminds you of the consequences or results of a command and asks you to confirm that you want to proceed with the action.

directory   A disk area that stores information about files. A directory is like a drawer in a file cabinet. Within that drawer, you can store several files.

directory tree A graphical display in a window of the directories on disk. The directory tree appears when you use the File Manager.

DOS An acronym for disk operating system. DOS manages the details of your system, such as storing and retrieving programs and files.

double-click The action of pressing the mouse button twice in rapid succession.

drag The mouse movement of pointing to an item and then pressing and holding the left mouse button as you move the mouse.

drop-down list box A box that lists the default choice in a dialog box. Other choices are available. To display the other choices, click the arrow in the square box at the right of the drop-down list box.

file The various individual reports, memos, databases, and letters that you store on your hard drive (or floppy diskette) for future use.

file name The name that you assign a file when you store it to disk. A file name consists of two parts: the root and the extension. The root can be up to eight characters long. The extension can be three characters long, and it usually indicates the file type. The root and extension are separated by a period. SALES.DOC is a valid file name. SALES is the root, and DOC is the extension.

format The initialization process that prepares a disk for use.

graphical user interface (GUI) A visual environment that enables you to learn a computer program more intuitively and to use a computer program more easily.

group A collection of programs. These programs are stored in a group window, which is represented by a group icon.

icon   An on-screen picture that represents a group window, an application, a document, or other elements within Microsoft Windows.

list box   A box within a dialog box that displays a list of items such as file names.

Maximize icon   The small up-arrow at the right of the title bar of a window.

menu bar   A list of menu names near the top of the window.

Minimize icon   The small down-arrow at the right of the window's title bar.

mouse pointer   The on-screen symbol that moves when you move the mouse. The pointer changes shape depending on which task you are performing, such as typing text, selecting a command, and so on.

open   The action of displaying the contents of a window on-screen.

option button   A round button that appears in a dialog box. To select an option, click in the option button. A dot appears in the button. You cannot activate more than one option button at a time.

path   The route, through directories, to a program or document file. The path C:\WINDOWS\TEMP\REPORT.DOC, for example, includes four elements: the disk drive (C:); the first directory (WINDOWS); the subdirectory, which is a directory within the first directory (TEMP); and the file name (REPORT.DOC).

root directory   The main directory. The root directory contains all other directories.

scroll bars   The bars at the bottom and right of a window. At the ends of the bars are scroll arrows; click on an arrow to scroll the window in the direction of the arrow.

text box A box within a dialog box. You type information—such as a file name—into the box to complete the command.

title bar The horizontal bar at the top of a window. The title bar contains the name of the window. Often, the title bar also contains the Control icon (at the left) and the Maximize and Minimize icons (at the right).

wild card Characters that stand for any other character that may appear in the same place. In Microsoft Windows, you can use the asterisk (*), which stands for any character (and any number of characters), and the question mark (?), which stands for any one character.

window A rectangular area on-screen in which you view an application or a document. A window can contain icons that represent applications, the application itself, or a document you have created in an application. Everything in Microsoft Windows is contained in a window.

Index